Automated Crime Information Systems

Automated Crime Information Systems

J. Van Duyn

TAB Professional and Reference Books

Division of TAB BOOKS
Blue Ridge Summit, PA

FIRST EDITION
FIRST PRINTING

© 1991 by TAB Professional and Reference Books, an imprint of TAB BOOKS.
TAB BOOKS is a division of McGraw-Hill, Inc.
The TPR logo, consisting of the letters "TPR" within a large "T," is a registered trademark of TAB BOOKS.

Printed in the United States of America. All rights reserved. The publisher takes no responsibility for the use of any of the materials or methods described in this book, nor for the products thereof.

Library of Congress Cataloging-in-Publication Data

Van Duyn, J. A., 1926-
   Automated crime information systems / by J. Van Duyn.
     p. cm.
   Includes bibliographical references.
   ISBN 0-8306-3503-3
   1. Information storage and retrieval systems—Criminal justice, Administration of—United States. 2. Criminal justice, Administration of—United States—Data processing. I. Title.
HV9950.V36 1990
364'.028'5—dc20   90-30672
                                                                   CIP

TAB BOOKS offers software for sale. For information and a catalog, please contact TAB Software Department, Blue Ridge Summit, PA 17294-0850.

Questions regarding the content of this book should be addressed to:

**Reader Inquiry Branch
TAB BOOKS
Blue Ridge Summit, PA 17294-0850**

Acquisitions Editor: Gerald T. Papke
Book Editor: Eileen P. Baylus
Production: Katherine G. Brown
Book Design: Jaclyn J. Boone

Contents

Acknowledgments *vii*
Preface *ix*
What This Book Will Do for You *xi*

1 Introduction *1*

2 National Crime Information Center (NCIC) *3*

3 Automated Identification System (AIS) and Interstate Identification Index (Triple I) *21*

4 Automated Fingerprint Identification Systems (AFIS) *29*

5 Criminal Justice Information Systems/Law Enforcement Telecommunication Systems *49*

6 Intellect Investigations System, United Crime Alert Network, Computer Aided Dispatch, and Other Software Applications *61*

7 Accessed Information, Privacy, Dignity, and Security Laws *71*

8 Computer Crime's Impact on Automated Systems *79*

9 Physical Security *87*

10	Hardware Security	*101*
11	Software Security	*111*
12	Personnel Security	*117*

Appendices

A	Western Identification Network, Inc.	*123*
B	Western Electronic Fingerprinting (Lifescan)	*125*
	Glossary	*129*
	Bibliography	*135*
	Index	*139*

Acknowledgments

Many people have contributed to this book with advice and information, and I am most grateful to all the law enforcement colleagues for their assistance. In addition, I owe a special debt of gratitude to Milt Ahlerich, Acting Assistant Director, U.S. Department of Justice, Federal Bureau of Investigation, Washington, D.C., and to John McMurdie, California Department of Justice, Sacramento, California. Mr. McMurdie reviewed and critiqued certain sections of the book, thus providing invaluable help.

J. Van Duyn

Preface

This book deals with the whole range of the automated crime information systems currently in use by United States criminal justice and law enforcement agencies.

Because there is no single source available for the criminal justice and law enforcement practitioners, university and college instructors, and students, this book is designed to be the sole, comprehensive reference on existing, in-progress, and planned automated crime information systems. Yet, no extraneous material is included just to make the book bulky or more impressive. Because criminal justice and law enforcement officers at all levels have neither the time nor the inclination to read boring, redundant text, the topic is presented as clearly and concisely as possible.

This book provides information on computer crime, as well as on the latest laws governing accessed information, privacy and security of data in the computer systems operated by federal, state, and local law enforcement agencies.

Some technical concepts are covered. These concepts include centralized versus decentralized database computer systems and how they work; and how criminal justice and law enforcement agencies utilize them. However, the orientation of the book is definitely nontechnical.

J. Van Duyn

What This Book Will Do for You

Whether you are a current or future law enforcement or criminal justice practitioner, this book will help you in your profession by providing you with data on the latest state-of-the-art automated crime information systems operated in the United States, as well as a large array of timely, related topics. To showcase the book, an overview of the subjects covered in each chapter and the reason you would want to know about it is presented here.

Chapter 1, "Introduction," gives you a bit of history about record-keeping systems that law enforcement agencies use, as well as the problems that automated crime information systems face in the criminal justice and law enforcement fields. It also tells you why it's important for both current and future law enforcement professionals to know more about computer crime, computer security, and laws covering privacy, security, and unauthorized accessing of sensitive data in law enforcement agencies' computer systems.

Chapter 2, "National Crime Information Center (NCIC)," provides you an in-depth description of the largest, most widely known automated crime information system in the country. For anybody in the law enforcement or criminal justice field, it's essential to know all about the FBI-operated NCIC with its thirteen giant databases and two subsystems.

Chapter 3, "Automated Identification System (AIS) and Interstate Identification Index (Triple I)," discusses in-depth NCIC's two subsystems. It presents a brief history and the function of each subsystem. It delves into the evolutionary process by which AIS, a huge repository that maintains the records of almost 100 million ten-print fingerprint cards and its accompanying criminal histories, became an automated system.

What This Book Will Do for You

It describes why and how Triple I, a cooperative effort by the FBI, the federal government, and the states that set up and maintain a unique system that deals solely with criminal offenders' history, came about. Triple I, while not a widely known computer system, is a great time-and-effort saver for all authorized agencies, and consequently an essential part of the automated crime information systems in this country.

Chapter 4, "Automated Fingerprint Identification Systems, (AFIS)," deals with the history, process, and subsequent automation of fingerprint comparison/matching and identification techniques of suspects used in all civilized countries. The California Department of Justice has the second largest fingerprint file in the country. The California Automated Identification System (CAL-ID) utilizes a cutting-edge computer system that is being used as a model nation- and world-wide. CAL-ID is discussed in-depth to show you an example of an efficiently working AFIS. Because CAL-ID is constantly evolving and expanding, the two planned, vastly different satellites—Western Identification Network (WIN) and DNA Database—are described as well.

Chapter 5, "Criminal Justice Information Systems (CJIS)/Law Enforcement Telecommunication Systems (LETS)," discusses two systems that are integral parts of all the automated crime information systems in this country. Actually, by now almost all 50 states have their own CJIS to keep track of criminals in their own states. Again, because the California CJIS—with seven databases and a very large subsystem—is one of the most sophisticated and comprehensive state systems in the country, it was chosen as an example. Without CJIS—and more specifically its subsystem, the Automated Criminal History System (ACHS)—that contains the Master Name Index (MNI) and interacts with the previously discussed CAL-ID—and also the Western States Information Network (WSIN) and Organized Crime Database, CAL-ID wouldn't be half as efficient as it is.

Furthermore, without the three law enforcement telecommunication systems—National Law Enforcement Telecommunications System (NLETS), International Law Enforcement Telecommunications System (INLETS), and California Law Enforcement Telecommunications System (CLETS)—no law enforcement or criminal justice agency would be able to access and retrieve information from any of the automated crime information systems in the United States, Canada, or overseas. Consequently, a knowledge of these two topics is essential to you, whether you are a current or future law enforcement practitioner.

Chapter 6, "Intellect Investigations System, United Crime Alert Network, Computer Aided Dispatch, and Other Software Applications" is a sampling of the hundreds if not thousands of computer applications that were designed for law enforcement. To appreciate these useful, field-tested computer software, each application is described in detail.

What This Book Will Do for You

Chapter 7, "Accessed Information, Privacy, Dignity, and Security Laws," contains facts that any person in law enforcement must know. This chapter provides a concise overview of laws that cover accessed information in law enforcement, government, and private computer systems. These laws include those that govern privacy, dignity, and security in all their forms, such as the fourth, fifth, and fourteenth amendments, the "bright line rules," the Exclusionary Rule, the Privacy Act of 1974, and the Freedom of Information Act of 1967.

Chapter 8, "Computer Crime's Impact on Automated Systems," is an area in the criminal justice and law enforcement fields that all practioners must know. Whether you are involved in investigating a computer crime or not, you should have some knowledge of the modus operandi of this purely twentieth century crime; its eight basic categories; and its potential perpetrators. There is also a discussion of the difference between "virus" and "worm."

Chapter 9, "Physical Security," is the building block on which an effective computer security program is built to counteract any and all types of computer crime in law enforcement, government, and commercial computer facilities. Physical security covers the outside of the facility, the lobby, security guards, ID badges/cards, intrusion detection devices, and proximity mode. But physical security is much more than that. It includes fire security and contingency and disaster recovery planning based on a comprehensive risk analysis. Because security measures are so important, you should have some concept of this and all the following computer crime countermeasures.

Chapter 10, "Hardware Security," is the second component of total security for automated crime information systems. Hardware security covers devices such as uninterruptible power supply (UPS) and off-site backup power generator. It also includes the various techniques to deter a potential perpetrator from accessing information via the office computer terminal. One of these techniques is the Biometric ID Systems, the latest techniques to effect maximum safety for sensitive data in law enforcement or criminal justice agencies' databases.

An extremely important and useful hardware security measure is the encryption system. Actually, there are two types of encryption systems: Data Encryption Standard (DES), which is used extensively by law enforcement, government, and large private organizations; and Public Key Encryption (PKE), which is not as well known or used as DES. Yet, interestingly both encryption systems use Message Authentication Code (MAC) technique, which further ensures the security and integrity of any message sent by cable, satellite, fiberoptics, or telephone.

Chapter 11, "Software Security," is the third component in establishing an effective computer crime prevention program. Software security, whether at a large- or medium-sized law enforcement or criminal justice

What This Book Will Do for You

agency, should include some kind of a software control system. There are several good control systems on the market. Resource Access Control Facility (RACF) is the most widely used in large computer centers by the FBI and federal and state department of justice facilities. Many smaller law enforcement agencies use The Repository, the latest sophisticated automated data dictionary system developed by IBM that does perhaps more than protect the software. Other types of software security techniques are described in this chapter.

Chapter 12, "Personnel Security," is the fourth and final component of a sound and comprehensive computer security strategy that law enforcement and criminal justice agencies should set up. Personnel security measures include a thorough background investigation, a cognitive team approach, and then a positive, objective personnel policy. Because in the majority of cases it is a disgruntled employee who is the perpetrator of a computer crime, possible indicators of discontentment as well as some field-tested practices to keep employees happy are discussed in this chapter.

Appendix A presents an update on the state-of-the-art Western Identification Network. Appendix B introduces Western Electronic Finger printing, or Lifescan, the very latest technique in using electronics to take a suspect's fingerprints. Lifescan is replacing the messy, and often smudged, ink-rolled fingerprinting across the country.

1
Introduction

In this era of increasing crime rate, quick access to timely and accurate information plays a key role in successful law enforcement activities. Thus, sophisticated automated crime information systems have become essential tools to criminal justice and law enforcement agencies.

Yet until the 1970s, federal, state, and local agencies used manual record-keeping systems to create and maintain criminal records. When a record was needed from a federal agency, both the request and the answer were sent by mail. As the volume of requests and the number of records increased, however, delays occurred in registering, obtaining, and updating the records. Because of the serious effects of these delays, the legislature made funds available to the FBI and other federal agencies—and subsequently to all the states—to automate their criminal record-keeping systems.

Criminal justice and law enforcement automated systems, however, face a set of problems that are unique. One of the problems is that an alarmingly large number of people in these fields either do not know anything about electronic data processing (EDP), or they are antagonistic toward computers. Others, who know something about EDP, have only a limited knowledge of the existing and developing automated criminal justice information systems.

Moreover, law enforcement practitioners who still have not completely accepted EDP are quick to point out that automated systems are prone to glitches or anomalies causing gaps of control that defense lawyers will circle like hungry vultures. Simply put, according to these persons, absolute reliance on automated systems insofar as perfect maintenance of a trail of evidence—an absolute necessity in criminal cases—is foolhardy. They say, "If an agency doesn't have a data processing department, it doesn't need one." Of course, they admit that good, reliable automated systems can be developed to speed processing, cata-

Introduction

loging, and locating evidence. But, they insist that a viable manual backup procedure is more than essential: it's imperative.

The second problem common to governmental agencies like law enforcement and criminal justice, is the fact that there tends to be overlapping responsibilities and redundant processes. A police department usually duplicates the services of a sheriff's office, which in turn duplicates the services of the state police. Many state services replicate services provided by the federal government. Each agency in each category has a database that it guards jealously. Such practice results in many databases collecting the same kind of information—a waste of resources at every level.

The third, and perhaps biggest, problem is that there is no single comprehensive source for criminal justice and law enforcement professionals, college and university criminal justice professors, and students about computerized information systems that are used currently by the federal, state, and local criminal justice and law enforcement agencies.

This book was written to fill this gap by providing an overview and then an in-depth discussion of all the automated crime information systems that are currently used or are being planned for the future. The content, structure, functions, and benefits of each system are presented, as well as the way it interacts with other crime information system(s), and the reasons you need to know about it.

Finally, all current and future law enforcement practitioners should be aware of the latest enacted federal and state laws governing privacy, security, and unauthorized accessing of sensitive information, and the latest computer crime modus operandi and countermeasures.

2

National Crime Information Center

Without a doubt, the largest and best-known automated crime information system—as well as one of the most effective crime-fighting tools for the past 20 years in the United States—is the National Crime Information Center (NCIC) located at FBI headquarters in Washington, D.C. This highly sophisticated system provides invaluable information on crime and criminals and is at the disposal of authorized state and local law enforcement and criminal justice agencies. Actually, NCIC is national in scope and designed to complement local criminal justice systems in the fifty states and U.S. possessions and territories.

Although the FBI is responsible for maintaining NCIC, the center is guided by an Advisory Policy Board. The board consists of twenty state law enforcement officials, six appointees of the Director of the FBI, and four representatives of national criminal justice professional associations such as the International Association of Chiefs of Police (IACP). The board members, who represent the four geographic regions of the United States, confer with state representatives, make recommendations, and formulate policies. The recommendations and new policies are then passed on to the Director of the FBI for his approval. Thus, in the final analysis, it is the director's decision as to NCIC's direction of operation, unless the U.S. Attorney General intercedes.

NCIC consists of a cluster of fourteen centralized-distributed type of databases and two subsystems. (See chapter 3.)

In a centralized-distributed database, while all the main processing of data is performed at the central location in a mainframe(s), information is entered, changed, added, and retrieved, but usually not deleted, through

National Crime Information Center (NCIC)

microcomputers and/or intelligent terminals located at various geographical locations. Generally, each different site maintains its own local database system, but users can and do communicate with each other. Users at any site can access data not only in the mainframe but anywhere in the network, just as if that data were in their own database system.

NCIC processes, stores, and disseminates information through telecommunications networks such as the National Law Enforcement Telecommunications System (NLETS), the California Law Enforcement Telecommunications System (CLETS), and the International Law Enforcement Telecommunications System (INLETS).

NCIC operates a separate database for each of the following categories of information: wanted persons; missing and unidentified persons; criminal offenders history (including fingerprints and forensic analyses); stolen and recovered property such as vehicles, boats, auto accessories, guns, heavy equipment, computers, cameras, household appliances, stolen and embezzled securities; Canadian warrants; U.S. Secret Service protective file; and Originating Agency Identification file.

NCIC is an *on-line system*, which means that it has the capability to retrieve or process information within seconds. Thus a patrol officer can input a request through his car's remote unit and receive a reply in a matter of seconds.

Note: The NCIC database used most by patrol officers across the country is the Wanted Persons database.

NCIC stores more than 18 million records and provides data to more than 60,000 authorized law enforcement and criminal justice agencies, in all of the fifty states and in the District of Columbia, Puerto Rico, U.S. possessions, and U.S. territories, as well as the Royal Canadian Mountain Police. Moreover, authorized college/university campus police and railroad police also can access certain NCIC databases.

BRIEF HISTORY OF FBI'S NCIC

In the 1960s, when law enforcement and criminal justice agencies became aware that computer technology can offer such benefits as providing timely data on crime and criminals, the FBI looked into the possibility of establishing a computerized index of information.[1] NCIC can be expanded and updated to keep up with the dynamically progressive high technology.

A typical instance of this system's expansion is the Computerized

---

[1] NCIC was established in accordance with Title 28, United States Code, Section 534, and Title 28 of the Code of Federal Regulations Judicial Administration, Chapter I—Department of Justice (Order No. 601-75) Part 20—Criminal Justice Information Systems, and put into operation in January 1967.

Criminal History (CCH) database, which was added to NCIC's cluster of databases in November 1971. CCH contains information concerning personal descriptions and fingerprints of individuals arrested for violations of serious crimes, the nature of crimes, and their disposition. NCIC is an outstanding example of how computer technology can help law enforcement officers become more effective through centralized, automated collecting and filing of vital information, and then communicating this information to local, state, and federal law enforcement and criminal agencies.

NCIC'S FOURTEEN DATABASES

It is important to remember that certain categories of records in each database have different retention periods. That is, after a predefined period they are deleted from the particular database to make room for additional records (See TABLE 2-1).

Wanted Persons

The Wanted Persons database holds descriptive profiles of wanted persons. Records in this database consist of the following details:

- The person's name and known aliases.
- The person's year of birth. (Age is crucial whenever career criminal statistics are gathered.)
- The offense for which the person was arrested.
- Date of Warrant/Last Contact.
- If the person was armed. (An *armed person* is any individual who has a weapon in his or her possession at the time of arrest. A weapon can be a gun, knife, baseball bat, or any object that can cause bodily harm.)
- Caution indicator. (This records whether the wanted person gave any forewarning of possible danger to the arresting officer(s).)
- Number of companions. (If there were any individuals with the wanted person at the time of arrest who consequently were arrested, detained, or investigated because of their association with the wanted person, it is to be recorded here.)
- Value of contraband recovered. (If there was any contraband recovered—contraband being anything that is illegal, such as drugs, and unregistered guns—its street value or fair market value is indicated here.)
- Value of property recovered. (If there was any property, such as stolen vehicle, equipment, money, and/or articles recovered, and the fair market value of such property.)

National Crime Information Center (NCIC)

Table 2-1. Retention Periods for Records in NCIC Databases.

Wanted Persons

- Temporary felony—48 hours
- All other wanted persons' records remain in the database until the originating agency removes it

Criminal History/FPC

- Temporary felony persons records —48 hours
- All other persons' records—including fingerprints—remain in the database until the originating agency removes it

Stolen & Recovered Guns

- Stolen guns remain in the database until removed by the originating agency
- Recovered gun—year when entered plus 2 years

Stolen & Recovered Boats & Marine Equip.

- Boat with hull identification number (HIN)—year when entered, plus 4 years
- Boat without HIN—90 days
- Marine equipment serial number— year when entered, plus 4 years

Stolen & Recovered Articles

- Stolen articles—year when entered plus 1 year
- Recovered articles—year when entered, plus 1 year

Missing Persons

- Automatic removal when missing juvenile reaches emancipation age
- All other missing persons' records remain in the database until the originating agency removes it

Stolen & Felony Vehicles

- Temporary felony vehicle—90 days
- Vehicle without vehicle identification number (VIN)—90 days
- Vehicle with VIN—year when entered, plus 4 years
- Aircraft with VIN—year when entered, plus 4 years
- Vehicle part serial number—year when entered, plus 4 years

Stolen & Recovered Heavy Equipment

- Equipment with VIN—year when entered, plus 4 years
- Recovered equipment—year when entered, plus 2 years

Stolen License Plates

- One year after expiration year of registration tag
- Nonexpiring registration tag—year when entered, plus 4 years

Stolen & Recovered Securities

- Stolen, embezzled, or counterfeited securities (except traveler's checks and money orders)—year when entered, plus 4 years
- Traveler's checks and money orders—year when entered, plus 2 years
- Recovered securities—year when entered, plus 2 years

Missing and Unidentified Persons

The Missing Persons database has been one of the components of NCIC since October 1, 1975. It gained added importance on October 12, 1982, when the Missing Children Act was signed into law. The act

NCIC's Fourteen Databases

requires the Attorney General to "acquire, collect and preserve any information which would assist in the location of any missing persons (including children, unemancipated persons as defined by the laws of the place of residence) and provide confirmation as to any entry (into NCIC records) for such a person to the parent, legal guardian or next of kin . . ."

In addition, the Missing Children Act allows the parent, legal guardian, or next of kin to directly request the FBI to check if data on a particular missing child has been entered into the NCIC. If no record on the missing child is found in the database, the FBI will notify the requestor. The FBI also will instruct the individual to contact the local law enforcement agency and find out why the agency did not enter the data on the missing child into NCIC. In certain cases the FBI is authorized to enter data into NCIC on a missing person when local law enforcement officers did not.

Moreover, if there is a *hit*—that is, if the FBI learns the missing person's location—the parent, legal guardian, or next of kin, and the local authorities will be notified immediately. However, the FBI is not empowered by the act to investigate the case of every missing child in the United States. The FBI is not responsible for detaining the missing child or returning the child to the parent, legal guardian, or next of kin.

If the missing child is kidnapped by a parent, the Federal Kidnapping Statute excludes the FBI from entering the case. It is to be handled by state and local authorities, unless one or more of the following apply (each case differs):

- The particular state issues a warrant charging the parent with a felony violation.
- There is solid evidence of interstate flight.
- The appropriate U.S. attorney authorizes the issuance of an unlawful flight warrant.
- There is a specific request for FBI assistance by the particular state.

The Missing Persons database is comprised of the following four distinct divisions:

Missing Disabled Persons. In this division are records of missing individuals who have physical and/or mental disability, such as senility, loss of memory, and so on.

Endangered Missing Persons. In this division are records of individuals who are missing and there is a good reason to suspect that they are in the company of other persons under circumstances indicating that their physical or mental safety is in danger.

National Crime Information Center (NCIC)

Involuntarily Missing Persons. In this division are records of individuals who are missing under circumstances that indicate an involuntary disappearance, such as in the case of abduction or kidnapping.

Missing Juvenile Persons. In this division are records of individuals who are missing and are declared unemancipated, as defined by the laws of their state of residence. Unemancipated means a minor who is under parental or legal guardian control until he/she reaches the age of maturity.

The Unidentified Persons database, which became operational on June 30, 1983, contains the following data about unidentified dead persons:

- Approximate age
- Sex
- Race
- Height
- Weight
- Eye and hair color
- Dental characteristics
- Broken bones, if any
- Other vital identification, such as impairment or abnormality

Any authorized agency staff members working on a missing person case can search the records in the Unidentified Persons database to check if there is a description of a deceased person in the database matching the description of the missing person.

If there is a "hit," the originating agency can request NCIC to erase that particular record in the Unidentified Persons and the Missing Persons databases. Then the investigator notifies the parent, legal guardian, or next of kin of the deceased person.

Criminal History and Fingerprint Classification

The Criminal History database contains comprehensive data on persons nationwide arrested for felony, murder, and other serious crimes, as well as the nature of the crime, and the disposition of the cases. Information in this database is often interchanged with NCIC's Wanted Persons database.

The Criminal History database consists of the following information:

- The person's name and known aliases.
- Year of birth. (As in the Wanted Persons database, age is crucial for gathering criminal statistics.)

- Crime. (The specific nature of the crime.)
- Date arrested.
- Disposition of the case. (Arraignment, date of trial, judgment, and sentence.)

The Fingerprint Classification (FPC) database collects and stores fingerprint classifications. Although not a positive identifier, the FPC can aid in completing the identity of a person in the Criminal History database. It also can help in establishing the identity of a suspect in the Wanted Persons database.

The Fingerprint Classification database uses the following fingerprint classification method that was selected for NCIC from many other fingerprint classification techniques:

- Pattern type (arch, loop, whorl, missing/amputated finger)
- Subgroup (plain, tented, radical, ulnar, plain whorl, inner tracing, central pocket loop, accidental whorl)
- FPC code (AA, TT, ridge count, P, PI, PM, CI, CM, D, XI)

To illustrate the advantage of employing the NCIC FPC, a set of fingerprints using the Henry System[2] would read:

No. 1 finger is an ulnar loop with 12 ridge counts; no. 2 finger has been amputated; no. 3 is a plain arch; no. 4 is a central pocket loop with other tracing; no. 5 is an ulnar loop with 4 counts; no. 6 is completely scarred; no. 7 is a radical loop with 9 ridge counts; no. 8 is a tented arch; no. 9 is a double loop with a meeting tracing; and no. 10 is an ulnar loop with 10 ridge counts.

Using the NCIC FPC, the same set of fingerprints would read:

12XXAAC004SR59TTdm10.

You can see the benefits of using NCIC FPC method—it saves time and space.

Stolen and Felony Vehicles

It is a well-known fact that automobiles, trucks, motorcycles, snowmobiles, and trailers are the favorite targets of thieves. When such thefts become part of organized crime, however, the rate of automobile theft can

---

[2]The HENRY System is a manual and rather slow fingerprint matching and identification process (*see* Glossary).

National Crime Information Center (NCIC)

soar alarmingly. Consequently, it is important to keep track of stolen vehicles and *felony vehicles*—vehicles used in the commission of a crime—in an easily accessible, up-to-date computer system. Nevertheless, consider that professional criminals who work on orders to steal automobiles for local and export markets are very well organized, thus effecting a low recovery rate and a high profit, low-risk crime.

The Stolen and Felony Vehicles database, in addition to stolen and felony vehicles, contains data on stolen aircraft. To add or inquire about a stolen or felony vehicle or stolen aircraft, the following specifics are needed:

- The originating state or federal agency case number
- Date of the transaction
- Vehicle or aircraft make and year
- Vehicle or aircraft license number (LIC), state, year, type
- Vehicle identification number (VIN)[3]
- Engine number
- Stolen vehicle
- Repossession
- Vehicle associated with a missing person
- Felony vehicle
- Vehicle reported lost
- Stored vehicle
- Impounded vehicle hold
- Stolen vehicle parts number

A hit in this database can provide information on other cases as well. It can provide information about stolen license plates, stolen vehicle parts, wanted persons, felony wanted persons, missing persons, missing juveniles, missing disabled person, endangered missing person, and involuntary missing persons.

A hit alone, however, usually is not sufficient legal grounds for *probable cause* to make an arrest (see glossary). When an inquiring agency staffer makes a hit, he or she must contact the originating agency (ORI) to verify all the data in the NCIC records. But if the hit on a stolen or felony vehicle is soon after the theft—and all the data is confirmed by the ORI—then the hit might be the only evidence needed to warrant probable cause.

Recovered Vehicles

When a stolen or felony vehicle or vehicle part is recovered by law enforcement officers anywhere in the country, this information is entered

---

[3] In 1984 a federal law was passed that requires a VIN to be stamped by the manufacturer on fourteen key parts of the automobile, including the transmission, doors, and bumpers.

NCIC's Fourteen Databases

into the NCIC Recovered Vehicles database. The data concerning the particular recovered vehicle is erased in the Stolen and Felony Vehicles and Vehicle Parts database.

The Recovered Vehicle database is comprised of information on the following:

- VIN and LIC of the vehicle recovered
- Date of recovery
- Value of vehicle recovered
- Person(s) apprehended in the course of recovering the vehicle, if any
- Case(s) cleared with the recovery, if any
- Value of contraband (anything illegal, such as drugs or unregistered guns) recovered, if any
- Value of other property (property or money taken during a robbery) recovered, if any
- Missing juvenile(s) located, if appropriate, as a result of recovering the stolen or felony vehicle
- Other missing person(s) located, if appropriate, as a result recovering the stolen or felony vehicle

Stolen and Recovered Firearms

The Stolen and Recovered Firearms database contains information on the following:

- Type of firearm
- Serial number of firearm
- Description of firearm
- Date of theft
- Date of recovery
- Person(s) apprehended in the course of recovering the gun(s), if any
- Case(s) cleared with the recovery of firearm(s), if any
- Value of contraband recovered, if any
- Value of other property recovered, if any
- Missing juvenile(s) located, if appropriate
- Other missing person(s) located, if appropriate

Stolen and Recovered Heavy Equipment

The dramatic rise of theft of construction and farm equipment across the country provides a serious problem to contractors, farmers, equipment manufacturers, and law enforcement officers. As with any other crime, the cost of such thefts ultimately falls on consumers. Theft increases construction cost, rent/lease cost, and produce cost.

National Crime Information Center (NCIC)

As in the case of stolen automobiles, the bulk of stolen heavy equipment can be attributed (perhaps even more so) to professional operators who steal on order for unscrupulous businessmen in this country as well as overseas. Such orders can be for stealing special components or parts of equipment—this means stripping the machine, or stealing the complete equipment for export. In any case, because these thefts are perpetrated by sophisticated, well-organized professional criminals, the recovery rate is very low. This, of course, makes theft of heavy equipment another high-profit, low-risk crime.

The Stolen and Recovered Heavy Equipment database contains the following information:

- Make and model of the equipment
- Serial number of the equipment
- Identification number of the equipment
- Serial and ID number of the equipment's components and attachments
- Value of the equipment
- Date of theft
- Date of recovery, if appropriate
- Person(s) apprehended, if any
- Case cleared, if appropriate

Stolen and Recovered Boats and Marine Equipment

Theft of boat and marine equipment is increasing at an alarming rate every year. Although local and state police and the harbor master might be the initial contact by victims of boat or marine equipment thefts, it is the Coast Guard that most often conducts the investigations. In fact, in June, 1977, the Coast Guard published the *Commandants Instruction No. 1620.3 and 16201.3* brochure. It defines the federal crimes involved in theft of boats and marine equipment, and establishes policies and procedures for the Coast Guard in investigating such crimes.

Commandants Instruction No. 16201.3 states:

(1) The Federal Crime of larceny (as set forth in T18 USC 661) consists of the 'taking' and the 'carrying away' of personal property with the intent to steal within the special maritime and territorial jurisdiction of the United States. The theft of a vessel does not, in itself, constitute a Federal crime, unless both the 'taking' and the 'carrying away' of the vessel occur within the jurisdiction.

(2) Breaking and entering a vessel with the intent to commit

a felony, if committed in the special maritime and territorial jurisdiction of the United States, is a Federal crime under T18 USC 2276.

(3) The theft of a vessel by its captain or any other member of its crew within the admiralty and maritime jurisdiction of the United States is a Federal crime under T18 USC 1656.

(4) The National Stolen Property Act, T18 USC 2314, prohibits the transportation of stolen goods valued at $5,000 or more in interstate or foreign commerce. Thus, it is a Federal crime to cross a state boundary with a stolen vessel which, together with its contents, is valued at $5,000 or more. In this context, a state's boundaries include not only its borders with other states, but also its maritime boundary, which coincides with the outer boundary of the territorial sea. Therefore, this Federal criminal statute is violated in one instance, when a stolen vessel of sufficient value is merely taken to the high seas beyond the territorial sea. Once the vessel has been removed from the state where it was stolen, a Federal crime has been committed, and returning the vessel to that state will not eliminate Federal jurisdiction.

(5) The Federal Boat Safety Act requires numbered vessels to have on board a valid certificate of number whenever the vessel is in use (T46 USC 1469 and 1483). If the genuine certificate of number is aboard a stolen vessel, and the operator of the vessel misrepresents himself to the Coast Guard as the owner, or as being in possession of the vessel with the permission of the owner, he violates T18 USC 1001. Likewise, presentation of a forged or altered certificate of number, or one obtained by misrepresenting the applicant as a lawful owner of the vessel, also constitutes a violation of T18 USC 1001.

The Commandants Instruction No. 1620.3, which defines policies and procedures for the Coast Guard in cases where no federal violation are involved, states:

(1) The Coast Guard may, in its law enforcement role, provide assistance to local and state law enforcement authorities under the provisions of T14 USC 141; or

(2) The Coast Guard may, in its role as protector of persons and property on the water, assist the vessel theft victim directly by helping locate his vessel.

Because the very nature of boats and marine equipment thefts affects jurisdictional problems among law enforcement agencies, and because these circumstances result in low recovery rate, this is still another high-profit, low-risk crime.

National Crime Information Center (NCIC)

The Stolen and Recovered Boats and Marine Equipment database contains the following information:

- Name of ORI
- Case number
- Date of theft
- Registration or document number of the boat and/or marine equipment
- Boat's hull identification number
- Type of boat (sailboat, motorboat, houseboat, yacht, etc.)
- Length and color of the boat
- Date of recovery

Stolen License Plates

A Stolen License Plates database was set up because of the widespread theft of license plates.

The Stolen License Plate database contains the following information:

- The originating agency case number
- Date of transaction
- Date of theft
- License number, state, year, and type
- Number of plates stolen
- If one plate still is on vehicle
- Miscellaneous—any additional data

Stolen and Recovered Securities

Theft and forging securities is not as well known a crime as stealing cars, boats, guns, and aircrafts, but it still occurs. Consequently, NCIC has a database specifically for this crime which, by the way, can often "earn" the perpetrator more money than the theft of an automobile. Stolen securities that can be entered into this NCIC database are serially numbered treasury and U.S. notes, bonds, and bills, municipal and corporate bonds, federal reserve notes, common and preferred stocks, and silver certificates.

The Stolen and Recovered Securities database contains the following information:

- Name of originating agency
- Case number
- Date of theft
- Security(s) registration number(s)

NCIC's Fourteen Databases

- Date of issuance
- Organization that issued the certificate(s)
- Date of recovery
- Miscellaneous—any additional data

Stolen and Recovered Identifiable Articles

For purposes of NCIC an *article* is an item of property that is identified by a serial number and not specified under other classifications. Articles that are entered in this database consist of the following: stolen and recovered auto accessories, avionic equipment (radios, navigation equipment, radar, and other electronic devices used in the operation of aircrafts), computers, cameras, tools, musical instruments, and office equipment.

The Article database consists of the following information:

- Originating agency case number
- Date of transaction
- Date of theft
- Name of article
- Value of article
- Date of recovery

Canadian Warrants

As a courtesy to the Royal Canadian Mounted Police, NCIC includes in its cluster of database systems a database dedicated to outstanding warrants of Canadian felons and other wanted persons. Data in this database is kept up to date by the Royal Canadian Mounted Police, who have access to all NCIC databases except its subsystem, Triple I. (This subsystem will be discussed in the next chapter.)

Information in this database can provide data on Canadian criminals with outstanding warrants who escape into the United States. Specifically, when a United States law enforcement officer makes an inquiry into this database and receives a hit, he can contact the Royal Canadian Mounted Police. However, because a Canadian warrant cannot be used in the United States as a basis for an arrest, the Canadian criminal justice officials have to initiate a process for a United States extradition warrant.

The Canadian Warrants database contains the following information:

- Name of originating agency (Royal Canadian Mounted Police)
- Case number
- Date of transaction
- Date of warrant
- Name of person on the warrant

National Crime Information Center (NCIC)

- Year of birth of person on the warrant
- Offense
- Caution indicator (If the person is known to be armed and dangerous.)

U.S. Secret Service Protective File

This highly confidential database was added to NCIC on April 27, 1983, after Congress approved it. It contains comprehensive histories of individuals considered of danger to present and past presidents, high officials, and visiting Heads of States. Until this database was set up, the Secret Service did not know the whereabouts of these individuals. Because of the high rate of hits in this computer system, it has become invaluable in locating such persons.

The information contained within this database is protected by a sophisticated cipher encryption system. The system, accessible only to selected authorized persons, relies heavily on its cryptographic algorithm and its unbreakable code.

Note: Cryptographic algorithm is a definitive set of computational procedures that performs a mathematical transformation within a finite number of structured steps. A cryptographic code is a specific combination of pattern of characters or numbers that converts intelligible information or data into unintelligible information or data, and vice versa.

Originating Agency Identifier File

The latest addition to the NCIC databases is the Originating Agency Identifier (ORI) File. It has over 56,000 records and continues to grow. The ORI File contains pertinent information on virtually every law enforcement and criminal justice agency in the United States, Canada, Puerto Rico, and U.S. Virgin Islands, as well as certain foreign criminal justice agencies, such as Scotland Yard.

An agency receiving an NCIC hit on a wanted or missing person or stolen property can make a single inquiry into the ORI File to find out the name, address, and telephone number of the agency that originated the record of the event. The important benefit of ORI File is that law enforcement and criminal justice agencies can use it to confirm any hit record with the originating agency.

NCIC'S MODE OF OPERATION.

The NCIC system uses several IBM 3033s host computers to support the 60,000 law enforcement and criminal justice agencies across the country. It operates under multiple virtual storage/system product (MVS/

SP) operating system (OS). Telecommunications support is provided by two Computer Communications, Inc. (CCI) CC-85 communications processors.

As stated earlier, data and information is exchanged between NCIC in Washington and authorized agencies nationwide online via microcomputers and intelligent terminals. NCIC records can be queried, updated, and modified, but not deleted by the authorized agencies.

NCIC is in operation twenty-four hours a day, seven days a week. It is always available to assist federal, state, and local agencies in the United States, as well as in its territories and possessions.

NCIC'S QUALITY CONTROL

To ensure that the records in NCIC's databases are accurate, complete, and timely, the agencies using this system must adhere to the policies and detailed procedures established by NCIC. In fact, because the NCIC policy clearly states that user agencies are responsible for the quality and integrity of the entered information, it is to the user agencies' benefit to follow the system rules in all transactions, including inquiry, entry, modification, or cancellation. For example, there is strict requirement that supporting documentation must be in the possession of the ORI before data is entered into NCIC in the following categories:

- An arrest warrant for a wanted person
- A missing person report for a missing person
- A theft report for a stolen car, boat, gun, article, and so on

As stated before, when a record is entered into any of the databases, it must contain a minimum of the following information: the identity of the ORI; the date of the transaction; the date of the warrant, or if it's about stolen property, the date of the theft; VIN, HIN, serial number, or registration number; and other definitive information. Moreover, all the data that is entered must be in the established order and format.

In addition, the NCIC system automatically edits all entries and modifications. These edits ensure that specific data is entered into the right place; that data is the right length; and that numerics are not entered into a field that was designed for letters or symbols. If the edits detect an error, the entry is rejected and a message specifying the error appears on the computer screen of the ORI.

Last but not least, NCIC implemented a nationwide audit program in 1984. The audit program assesses quality of data and accuracy of data entered and maintained by the states and originating agencies, and monitors the states' compliance with established NCIC policies.

National Crime Information Center (NCIC)

SECURITY AND PRIVACY

Security and privacy of data entered and maintained in the NCIC databases is ensured by the following strict NCIC requirements:

- New records can be entered into one of the databases only by the ORI that is directly involved with the criminal, the offense, or the particular event (missing person) that provides the basis for the entry of a new record.
- Before a terminal operator can make an inquiry, entry, modification, or cancellation, into any NCIC database, he must supply the system a NCIC-assigned ORI ID number, identifying the originating agency. He also must give his authorization code.
- User agencies must cross check, whenever possible, about new data to be entered into NCIC. For example, in case of a reported stolen or felony vehicle, the VIN and LIC must be verified with state departments of motor vehicles.
- Before a new record is entered into NCIC by a terminal operator, the case officer or a supervisor must verify that the data to be entered into the system is accurate. It must match the data in the investigative report and/or other source documents.

LONG-RANGE GOALS OF NCIC

From the start, NCIC's long-range goal was "to provide for the compilation, dissemination, and exchange of time-critical criminal justice and law enforcement information." In July 1987, the Advisory Policy Board—which together with the FBI manages NCIC—awarded a two-year contract to a consulting firm to study and formulate recommendations for a comprehensive modernization and expansion or replacement of the current NCIC by the year 2000. The recommendations will be considered carefully by the FBI and the Advisory Policy Board prior to submitting it to Congress.

The following requirements are to be included in the recommendations for the NCIC 2000 System:

- Design, develop, and implement a new, additional database to track and record the movements of individuals on parole or probation, convicted terrorists, foreign spies, and people under criminal investigation across state lines
- List the known group membership of wanted individuals in the same new database
- Add misdemeanors and juveniles crimes to NCIC's Criminal History database

Long-Range Goals of NCIC

- Add the ability to transmit by telecommunications photographs, fingerprints, signatures, and other images
- Improve the search capabilities of NCIC to increase the number of hits from a query by adding the capability of being able to search by nickname and/or by modus operandi of a wanted person
- Establish online telecommunications to databases at the Securities and Exchange Commission, the Social Security Administration, and other federal agencies.

3

Automated Identification System and Interstate Identification Index

NCIC has two subsystems: Automated Identification System (AIS) and Interstate Identification Index (Triple I). AIS is an automated version of FBI's manual identification division system that was established in 1924 by the FBI as the nation's central repository and clearinghouse for fingerprint records and biographical data of identified criminals. Back in those days, when a person was arrested or applied for a job at any law enforcement or criminal justice agency or other government agencies, or when an individual was seeking a license to sell liquor, establish private security services, or open a daycare center, the FBI's identification division was the primary source for checking if the person had a criminal record in any state. Because states usually have records of criminal activities that occur only within their own state, it was the FBI's identification division that provided all authorized requesting agencies fingerprint records and biographical data of criminals nationwide.

The Triple I system is based on a concept of shared FBI and state responsibility suggested in April 1978 by NCIC users, approved by the Advisory Policy Board, and developed by the FBI in 1981. It became operational in February, 1983. Triple I, unlike AIS, was designed and developed for officials to enter, maintain, and disseminate solely criminal offenders' history records. In addition, it was set up so that not only authorized state and federal agencies, as well as licensing boards, banks, financial institutions, and school systems, can access it to check job or license applicants' background for possible criminal records.

AIS & Interstate Identification Index

BRIEF HISTORY OF
AUTOMATED IDENTIFICATION SYSTEM

With the startup in 1924 of the identification division system, the FBI laid the first building block toward a comprehensive crime information system to assist law enforcement and criminal justice agencies across the country and beyond.

Subsequently, because the files in this manual system increased to 10 million by 1939 and kept increasing with each year and because the concept of computers and automation started to be accepted, the FBI decided to computerize its identification division. After lengthy planning and discussion periods, the budget for automating the identification division was approved by Congress. In 1975, the FBI began the first phase of the monumental task of automating this manual system, by then containing some 45 million fingerprints and biographical data on cards. In 1983 the second phase of AIS was implemented and then connected with NCIC. By that time, AIS computer databases contained some 83 million criminal fingerprint and biographical data records. The final, third phase of AIS is being implemented.

Note: To eliminate duplication of AIS and Triple I records, plans are to merge AIS with Triple I as soon as the final phase of AIS is completed.

STRUCTURE AND FUNCTIONS OF AIS

Initially, the reason for automating the FBI's identification division was to improve the service to law enforcement and criminal justice agencies such as police, courts, and parole officials. By computerizing the millions of 10-print fingerprint cards, the processing and responding time was reduced substantially. Moreover, in the process, new technologies evolved that were utilized to enhance the total system.

Thus, not only was the reading and processing of fingerprints automated, but the accompanying criminal history records as well. AIS was able to reduce the response time to online requests for records in this database system from the original period of two to three weeks to less than eighteen hours for most requests. AIS staff members, because of Triple I, were able to concentrate on receiving, processing, matching, and responding to fingerprint identification requests.

Traditionally, the requests were submitted on cards with the individual's fingerprints, as well as the person's name, social security number, height, and weight. If AIS came up with a "hit" it transmitted a copy or *rap sheet* of the individual's criminal record to the requesting authorized party.

As a side benefit to automating AIS, a new, better, and faster technique is emerging to identify crime scene latent fingerprints. This new method developed by the FBI is called *Automated Latent System Model (ALSM)*.

Before describing ALSM in detail, it is better to discuss the detecting and lifting techniques used to get latent fingerprints at a crime scene. To begin with, when a person touches anything with his finger, it leaves a residue of amino acids, water, oil, salt, and other chemicals in the lines, swirls, and ridge characteristics (minutiae) at the fingertips. One of the methods of detecting and lifting prints is carbon dusting powder. This technique, however, works only on hard surfaces, such as glass and metal. It does not work on any kind of porous material, such as fabric and paper, because porous surfaces absorb the residue of human skin. Consequently, until the advent of new techniques, most latent prints lifted by dusting powder were quite useless.

Current detecting and lifting methods include the use of chemicals and lasers. The most recent and most effective chemical used for fingerprint detecting and lifting is cyanoacrylate, known as the superglue in most households. Cyanoacrylate is effective on various fabrics and plastics. Lasers are being used when neither dusting powder nor chemicals are effective in detecting and lifting latent prints at a crime scene. A handheld laser scanner can flood material with an intense green light. The scanner can pick up fingerprint residue that might not be seen by the human eye. The latent fingerprint is photographed and processed by ALSM.

When the total ALSM system is completed and in production mode by the early 1990s, it will be a truly high-tech, cutting edge *expert system* based on artificial intelligence concepts. Because artificial intelligence is a field of study generally concerned with making a computer system emulate human thinking, ALSM—based on artificial intelligence—will imitate the human decision process in classifying and identifying fingerprints.

ALSM will be able to effect such processing because expert systems' main features include a decision process, and decision-making according to rule-based knowledge. More precisely:

- An expert system's decision process is based on fundamental knowledge given to the computer system about a specific subject.
- An expert system is able to arrive at a decision because it is provided with the rule-based knowledge or rule of thumb that an expert in the field would employ to make decisions. Thus, expert systems can solve problems, or in this case, classify fingerprints as human experts would.

The first phase of the project concerns a pilot automatic fingerprint reader system. This experimental automatic fingerprint reader has the capability to do online searching and matching against the AIS fingerprint database of repeat offenders in specific crime categories. More precisely, the automatic fingerprint reader scans the minutiae characteristics to identify a fingerprint. Then the system reviews candidates whose personal and crime profile possibly match, and finally ALSM compares all likely candidates' fingerprints with the particular latent fingerprint through its matching algorithm, i.e., computer program.

To test the accuracy of the pilot automatic fingerprint reader—that is, to check if it is properly matching latent prints with fingerprints retrieved from AIS database—a rigorous verification procedure takes place. One expert fingerprint examiner analyzes and determines whether the two prints are identical, and a second examiner verifies if the determination is correct. This underlines the fact that regardless of how sophisticated computer systems are, human beings still are needed to make final decisions, at least in the experimental stages.

The ALSM project—now in progress—consists of the following three phases:

Phase 1. The (Pilot) Automated Fingerprint Reader System. This complex pilot system, when in production mode, will be able to read, classify, identify, and store even partial and smudged fingerprints.

Phase 2. The Automated Image Retrieval System (AIRS). This system will receive fingerprints through telecommunications systems. It will eliminate the current slow method of sending fingerprint cards through the mail and entering the cards into AIRS through an optical character reader (OCR) or some other device. Once the fingerprints are received, they will be transmitted to the Automated Fingerprint Reader for processing. If AIRS finds the fingerprints too illegible to be classified and identified by the Automated Reader, it will direct the fingerprints to a staff expert examiner instead of the computer system.

In addition, through AIRS the AIS examiner staff will be able—within minutes—to retrieve fingerprints stored in the AIS database and display them on the terminal's screen.

Phase 3. Phase 3 is the incorporation and implementation of the first two systems into a total ALSM production system.

BRIEF HISTORY OF TRIPLE I

In the late 1960s and early 1970s several states became frustrated by the delays in obtaining data from the FBI's identification division. They asked the FBI to do something about it.

The problem the FBI had to solve was compounded by the growing number—6 million annually—of requests for criminal history records by law enforcement and criminal justice agencies, state licensing agencies, and employers. At the same time, the volume of criminal fingerprint and biographical data that had to be entered and maintained increased tenfold.

AIS & Interstate Identification Index

In those days requests to the FBI for criminal records, as well as responses, were sent by mail—a rather slow and tedious method.

What evolved out of the analysis and consequent lengthy consideration of several proposed solutions was the Triple I. Triple I, developed by the FBI and partly funded by the federal government and by some states, is managed jointly by the FBI and participating states. Participating states are states whose officials sign an *information access agreement* with NCIC, pay a $36,000 start up cost, and a $2,300 to $3,000 monthly operating cost. These officials can utilize this sophisticated *centralized computer information system*.

Triple I saves a lot of money to all parties. Specifically, by transmitting records through NLETS to requesting agencies rather than mailing the responses realizes an estimated savings of 29 cents for each record sent. Participating states also realize savings by eliminating manual updating of files in recording new FBI Criminal Identification and Information (CII) numbers, and/or new State Identification (SID) numbers.

The officials of participating states* have primary responsibility for maintaining and disseminating detailed criminal offenders' history records of their own state. In addition, whenever there is an arrest in the twenty-one currently participating states, a record and two fingerprint cards are prepared. The two cards are sent to the State Identification Bureau for processing.

Once a SID number is assigned, one card is entered and retained at the originating state's Criminal History database; the second card is sent to NCIC's Triple I. If there is no prior record of the person in NCIC's Triple I databases, the FBI assigns a CII number before adding it to its databases. That is how NCIC's Triple I is able to maintain an automated index of the location of all Triple I records. As of April 1987, NCIC entered and stored indices of almost 11 million state criminal history records in its Triple I databases. This amount, by the way, is steadily increasing with each year.

NCIC's Triple I database allows NCIC to provide authorized requestors information as to which state has in its files the particular person's record. NCIC also notifies the appropriate state officials when a criminal history record is requested, so that the officials are aware that there will be a request for that record.

Note: State employees send requests and receive responses from NCIC's Triple I through NLETS. This telecommunication system is located in Phoenix, Arizona, and run by a board composed of a group of

---

*The participating states include: California, Colorado, Florida, Georgia, Idaho, Kansas, Michigan, Minnesota, Missouri, Nebraska, Nevada, New Jersey, New York, North Carolina, Ohio, Oregon, Pennsylvania, South Carolina, Texas, Virginia, Washington, and Wyoming.

states law enforcement agency personnel. Actually, NLETS is nothing more than a message switching system. It transmits requests and responses between NCIC and the appropriate states. It is an easy to use yet quite sophisticated and very efficient tool for communication. The few states that still have not automated their manual systems, of course, have to send requests and receive responses through the mail.

TRIPLE I'S STRUCTURE AND FUNCTIONS

Triple I is used by federal, state, and local law enforcement and criminal justice agencies, in addition to authorized state licensing boards, banks, financial institutions, and schools. Its importance can be measured by the fact that according to the FBI at least 65 percent of all persons arrested are repeat offenders, and of these, 33 percent have criminal records in more than one state. Thus, in trying to stem the increase of criminal activities nationwide, it is essential to share criminal history records across jurisdictional boundaries. Such sharing has been made very easy through a single check (using NLETS) to Triple I. Simply put, an inquiring organization can quickly determine, by accessing Triple I via NLETS, whether a suspect, a job applicant, or a license applicant has a criminal record in any state of the union or in NCIC.

Curiously, if an authorized organization staff member in California (or any participating state) sends a request for information about an individual's criminal record in his own state to Triple I in Washington, it will be denied. NCIC will refuse to give any information, and the requestor will be told to access his own state's criminal history system for the information he needs. Participating states can access other state's criminal history systems through Triple I via NLETS, and authorized Canadian agencies can access participating states' criminal history systems through International Law Enforcement Telecommunications System (INLETS). This is not the case for authorized organizations within their own states.

In California, for example, authorized agencies have to access Automated Criminal History System (ACHS)—an important component of Criminal Justice Information System (CJIS)—via CLETS to obtain information about an individual's criminal record.

For any authorized state user to get information about an individual from any state's criminal history system, the original request goes via NLETS to NCIC's Triple I in Washington. This rerouting serves two purposes:

1. Because NCIC's Triple I maintains an index of where the detailed records of all criminal offenders' histories are, it can in seconds direct the requestor to the state(s) where he can get the needed

data. (Thus NCIC saves the requestor time and money in not contacting all participating states.)
2. NCIC can keep an audit trail of how many requests are sent, who is requesting data, and the frequency of the requests. NCIC will allow only agencies who signed an information access agreement with NCIC to use the Triple I system.

USERS AND USAGE OF TRIPLE I

Police and sheriff investigators can use the data in Triple I to develop leads; prosecutors can use it in presenting criminal charges to the court; courts can use it in bail and sentencing decisions; and parole boards can use it in making a determination about offender participation in various institutional or release programs. State licensing boards can use the data in granting licenses; and banks, financial institutions, and school systems use it in checking job applicants.

To use Triple I, the request from authorized organizations must contain the unique CII number, or SID number, or the individual's name to obtain a subject's criminal character portrait from a participating state Triple I and/or NCIC's Criminal History database.

Note: To date, besides the FBI, California and New York are the only criminal justice agencies that require a fingerprint card with a request before providing any criminal history on an individual.

Responses by Triple I include the name, aliases, sex, race, date of birth, height, weight, social security number, and unique identifiers (such as a tattoo, scars) of each person who has a criminal record in any state that participates in this system.

The Triple I records contain the arrest(s) and disposition of cases as well as fingerprint references. Triple I can provide only fingerprint references, while AIS can supply a complete fingerprint profile of all identified criminals in its database. Consequently, if a positive identification, or "hit," is made to an inquiry by one of the participating state's Triple I, the requesting agency can decide whether to ask AIS for fingerprints.

A new record entered into a participating state's criminal history system must be supported by data on duplicate tenprint cards filled out at the time of arrest. One card is retained by the particular state, and the second is sent to AIS, which then supplies the essential data to NCIC's Triple I for indexing. This procedure is in line with the agreement between the two parties stating that individual states are the primary holders of their own criminal history records, while the FBI, stores and maintains an index of all participating states' records.

If, however, no prior fingerprint record is in the AIS database about the individual whose criminal history is requested, a CII number is assigned to the fingerprint card and thus recorded in AIS. The CII number is then transmitted to NCIC's Triple I database for indexing.

PRIVACY AND SECURITY

Because it is essential that data entered into Triple I is both accurate and complete, a nationwide quality assurance measure was enacted. If data in Triple I is erroneous or incomplete, untold damage can result because information is accessed by so many parties: criminal justice agencies, government and commercial agencies, and private individuals.

To ensure privacy and security of data in Triple I, participating state officials sign an agreement with the FBI. This document mandates that the participating states will do the following:

1. Conform to the established rules, policies, procedures, and security measures established by the FBI in operating Triple I. These policies include guidelines as to who can access Triple I; the authorization levels for users in Triple I; and so on.
2. Require all organization personnel using Triple I in their state sign a similar agreement.
3. Require all transactions to be logged by the computer, so that there is an audit trail for verification.

In addition, twice a year the FBI sends to the participating states a tape that contains the index of their own criminal history records for auditing and validating purposes. Thus, discrepancies can be corrected both in the states' records and in NCIC's Triple I database, when the corrected tapes are returned to the FBI.

4

Automated Fingerprint Identification Systems (AFIS)

Based upon the scientific fact that fingerprints are unique to each person, for almost a century law enforcement agencies have been using manual fingerprint comparison as an effective way of identifying a suspect. The manual process of comparing and identifying fingerprints—either from fingerprints rolled in ink and pressed upon *10-print cards* (a card with all ten fingers imprinted on it), or latent (left behind, hidden) fingerprints found and lifted at a crime scene—is called the *Henry System*. The system was named after an Englishman, Sir Edward Richard Henry, who was commissioner of London's Metropolitan Police in the 1880s. Commissioner Henry developed a fingerprint classification system where a numeric code, based on the placement of whorl patterns among the ten fingers, was combined with alpha codes representing the patterns of the remaining ten fingers, and ridge counts between core and delta, or delta and delta, for the thumbs and little fingers. *Core* is the center point of the fingerprint. Basically, it is the top of the innermost *recurving* ridge. *Delta* is the triangle where the ridge lines divide or separate. Delta occurs in both whorls and loops, but not in arch patterns.) The fingerprint cards were stored according to the resulting composite code with breakdowns within the more common of the codes by age and sex. With minor modifications, this manual system is still in use at many law enforcement agencies in English-speaking countries. (See FIG. 4-1.)

With the advent of electronic data processing, however, automated fingerprint matching and identification systems have evolved. In the high-tech fingerprint matching and identification process the ridge detail of the

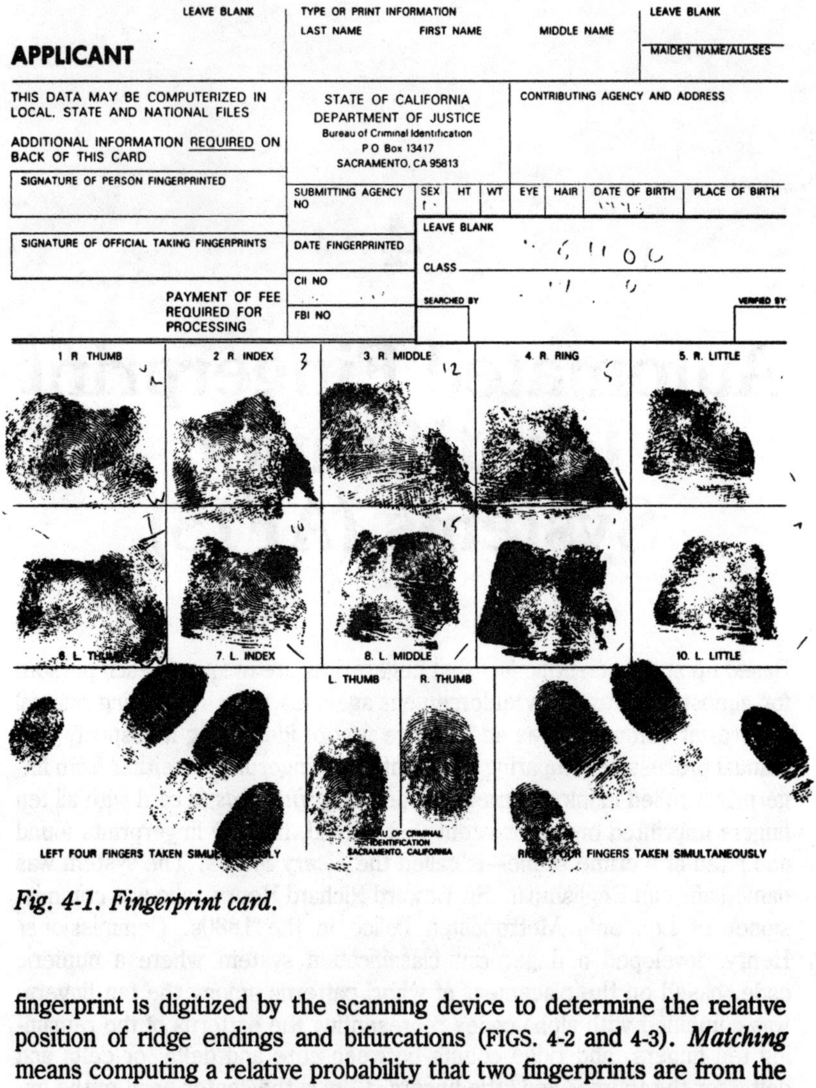
LEAVE BLANK
APPLICANT
TYPE OR PRINT INFORMATION
LAST NAME FIRST NAME MIDDLE NAME
LEAVE BLANK
MAIDEN NAME/ALIASES
THIS DATA MAY BE COMPUTERIZED IN LOCAL, STATE AND NATIONAL FILES
ADDITIONAL INFORMATION REQUIRED ON BACK OF THIS CARD
STATE OF CALIFORNIA
DEPARTMENT OF JUSTICE
Bureau of Criminal Identification
P O Box 13417
SACRAMENTO, CA 95813
CONTRIBUTING AGENCY AND ADDRESS
SIGNATURE OF PERSON FINGERPRINTED
SUBMITTING AGENCY NO
SEX HT WT EYE HAIR DATE OF BIRTH PLACE OF BIRTH
LEAVE BLANK
SIGNATURE OF OFFICIAL TAKING FINGERPRINTS
DATE FINGERPRINTED
CLASS
CII NO
PAYMENT OF FEE REQUIRED FOR PROCESSING
SEARCHED BY
VERIFIED BY
FBI NO
1 R THUMB
2 R INDEX
3 R MIDDLE
4 R RING
5 R LITTLE
6 L THUMB
7 L INDEX
8 L MIDDLE
10 L LITTLE
L THUMB
R THUMB
LEFT FOUR FINGERS TAKEN SIMULTANEOUSLY
RIGHT FOUR FINGERS TAKEN SIMULTANEOUSLY

Fig. 4-1. Fingerprint card.

fingerprint is digitized by the scanning device to determine the relative position of ridge endings and bifurcations (FIGS. 4-2 and 4-3). *Matching* means computing a relative probability that two fingerprints are from the same finger (of a subject) by comparing the relative positions of these *minutiae*, the unique ridges/lines and swirls at the end of the finger.

An average finger has about 100 minutiae; a large finger can have up to 150 minutiae. According to fingerprint experts, eight corresponding minutiae points in any given fingerprint have a high probability of a match or "hit" with a database-stored fingerprint, if that fingerprint exists in the database. Thus, while the manual Henry System only has a 75% hit rate, the computerized minutiae system has a 93% hit rate.

To understand the importance of the fingerprint matching and identifying process, it is time to clarify what constitutes a fingerprint. To begin with, the epidermal cells of the skin on fingers grow in patterns composed

Automated Fingerprint Identification Systems (AFIS)

```
*AFIS*             DESCRIPTIVE INFORMATION & IMAGE SCREEN      09/28/89 15:23
                   DPF: DISPLAY FILE-PRINT DATA (TENPRINT)     PCN: 28-0-0285-6
                             (8 FINGERS/CARD)
   OPERATOR ID: HILBURN
   TERMINAL ID: F002

   KEY NO.         : 085-000-013
   SEX             : M
   YOB / RANGE     : 45 / 0
   DOA             : ??/??/??
   CRIME           :
   CONTRIBUTOR     : ??
   REGION CODE     : ??
   MEMO            :
   PATTERN TYPE    : W R R R R - W R L L L
   (QUALITY)       : A B B B * - B B B B *
   RDB-T FINGERS:  1,6
   DIDB FLAG       : Y
   FLAGS           : MA/NS/AP/LC

   ORIG.OP.ID: HILBURN
   ORIG.T.ID : F002
   INPUT DATE: 09/28/89                         FINGER NO.: 01


*AFIS*             DESCRIPTIVE INFORMATION & IMAGE SCREEN      09/28/89 15:24
                   DPF: DISPLAY FILE-PRINT DATA (TENPRINT)     PCN: 28-0-0285-6
                             (8 FINGERS/CARD)
   OPERATOR ID: HILBURN
   TERMINAL ID: F002

   KEY NO.         : 085-000-013
   SEX             : M
   YOB / RANGE     : 45 / 0
   DOA             : ??/??/??
   CRIME           :
   CONTRIBUTOR     : ??
   REGION CODE     : ??
   MEMO            :
   PATTERN TYPE    : W R R R R - W R L L L
   (QUALITY)       : A B B B * - B B B B *
   RDB-T FINGERS:  1,6
   DIDB FLAG       : Y
   FLAGS           : MA/NS/AP/LC

   ORIG.OP.ID: HILBURN
   ORIG.T.ID : F002
   INPUT DATE: 09/28/89                         FINGER NO.: 02


*AFIS*             DESCRIPTIVE INFORMATION & IMAGE SCREEN      09/28/89 15:24
                   DPF: DISPLAY FILE-PRINT DATA (TENPRINT)     PCN: 28-0-0285-6
                             (8 FINGERS/CARD)
   OPERATOR ID: HILBURN
   TERMINAL ID: F002

   KEY NO.         : 085-000-013
   SEX             : M
   YOB / RANGE     : 45 / 0
   DOA             : ??/??/??
   CRIME           :
   CONTRIBUTOR     : ??
   REGION CODE     : ??
   MEMO            :
   PATTERN TYPE    : W R R R R - W R L L L
   (QUALITY)       : A B B B * - B B B B *
   RDB-T FINGERS:  1,6
   DIDB FLAG       : Y
   FLAGS           : MA/NS/AP/LC

   ORIG.OP.ID: HILBURN
   ORIG.T.ID : F002
   INPUT DATE: 09/28/89                         FINGER NO.: 03
```

Fig. 4-2. Scanned fingerprints with identification system.

Automated Fingerprint Identification Systems

```
*AFIS*              DESCRIPTIVE INFORMATION & IMAGE SCREEN    09/28/89 15:25
                    DPF: DISPLAY FILE-PRINT DATA (TENPRINT)   PCN: 28-0-0285-6
                               (8 FINGERS/CARD)

     OPERATOR ID: HILBURN
     TERMINAL ID: F002

     KEY NO.        : 085-000-013
     SEX            : M
     YOB / RANGE    : 45 / 0
     DOA            : ??/??/??
     CRIME          :
     CONTRIBUTOR    : ??
     REGION CODE    : ??
     MEMO           :
     PATTERN TYPE   : W R R R R - W R L L L
     (QUALITY)      : A B B B * - B B B B *
     RDB-T FINGERS: 1,6
     DIDB FLAG      : Y
     FLAGS          : MA/NS/AP/LC

     ORIG.OP.ID: HILBURN
     ORIG.T.ID : F002
     INPUT DATE: 09/28/89                      FINGER NO.: 04


*AFIS*              DESCRIPTIVE INFORMATION & IMAGE SCREEN    09/28/89 15:25
                    DPF: DISPLAY FILE-PRINT DATA (TENPRINT)   PCN: 28-0-0285-6
                               (8 FINGERS/CARD)

     OPERATOR ID: HILBURN
     TERMINAL ID: F002

     KEY NO.        : 085-000-013
     SEX            : M
     YOB / RANGE    : 45 / 0
     DOA            : ??/??/??
     CRIME          :
     CONTRIBUTOR    : ??
     REGION CODE    : ??
     MEMO           :
     PATTERN TYPE   : W R R R R - W R L L L
     (QUALITY)      : A B B B * - B B B B *
     RDB-T FINGERS: 1,6
     DIDB FLAG      : Y
     FLAGS          : MA/NS/AP/LC

     ORIG.OP.ID: HILBURN
     ORIG.T.ID : F002
     INPUT DATE: 09/28/89                      FINGER NO.: 06
```

Fig. 4-2. Continued.

of lines, whorls, ridges, and valleys. The ridges serve a useful purpose: they keep the skin from sliding when pressed against another surface.

Sweat and oil, produced in the subcutaneous layer below the epidermis, as well as dust and grease, collect in the valleys between the ridges. When the ridged skin is pressed against any surface, some of this viscous material is transferred to the surface, and an impression of the ridge-and-valley patterns with minutiae points is left behind. Ridge patterns and minutiae points are unique to each individual, as is the space between minutiae points. An impression found on a given surface and matched with a suspect's fingerprint will prove legally that the suspect touched that surface.

This type of fingerprint is called a *latent print* because it is not visible to the naked eye. A latent print does not indicate the sex, age, or race of

Automated Fingerprint Identification Systems (AFIS)

```
*AFIS*              DESCRIPTIVE INFORMATION & IMAGE SCREEN         09/28/89 15:26
                    DPF: DISPLAY FILE-PRINT DATA (TENPRINT)        PCN: 28-0-0285-6
                              (8 FINGERS/CARD)
    OPERATOR ID: HILBURN
    TERMINAL ID: F002

    KEY NO.          : 085-000-013
    SEX              : M
    YOB / RANGE      : 45 / 0
    DOA              : ??/??/??
    CRIME            :
    CONTRIBUTOR      : ??
    REGION CODE      : ??
    MEMO             :
    PATTERN TYPE     : W R R R R - W R L L L
    (QUALITY)        : A B B B * - B B B B *
    RDB-T FINGERS: 1,6
    DIDB FLAG        : Y
    FLAGS            : MA/NS/AP/LC

    ORIG.OP.ID: HILBURN
    ORIG.T.ID : F002
    INPUT DATE: 09/28/89                          FINGER NO.: 07
```

```
*AFIS*              DESCRIPTIVE INFORMATION & IMAGE SCREEN         09/28/89 15:26
                    DPF: DISPLAY FILE-PRINT DATA (TENPRINT)        PCN: 28-0-0285-6
                              (8 FINGERS/CARD)
    OPERATOR ID: HILBURN
    TERMINAL ID: F002

    KEY NO.          : 085-000-013
    SEX              : M
    YOB / RANGE      : 45 / 0
    DOA              : ??/??/??
    CRIME            :
    CONTRIBUTOR      : ??
    REGION CODE      : ??
    MEMO             :
    PATTERN TYPE     : W R R R R - W R L L L
    (QUALITY)        : A B B B * - B B B B *
    RDB-T FINGERS: 1,6
    DIDB FLAG        : Y
    FLAGS            : MA/NS/AP/LC

    ORIG.OP.ID: HILBURN
    ORIG.T.ID : F002
    INPUT DATE: 09/28/89                          FINGER NO.: 08
```

```
*AFIS*              DESCRIPTIVE INFORMATION & IMAGE SCREEN         09/28/89 15:26
                    DPF: DISPLAY FILE-PRINT DATA (TENPRINT)        PCN: 28-0-0285-6
                              (8 FINGERS/CARD)
    OPERATOR ID: HILBURN
    TERMINAL ID: F002

    KEY NO.          : 085-000-013
    SEX              : M
    YOB / RANGE      : 45 / 0
    DOA              : ??/??/??
    CRIME            :
    CONTRIBUTOR      : ??
    REGION CODE      : ??
    MEMO             :
    PATTERN TYPE     : W R R R R - W R L L L
    (QUALITY)        : A B B B * - B B B B *
    RDB-T FINGERS: 1,6
    DIDB FLAG        : Y
    FLAGS            : MA/NS/AP/LC

    ORIG.OP.ID: HILBURN
    ORIG.T.ID : F002
    INPUT DATE: 09/28/89                          FINGER NO.: 09
```

Fig. 4-3. Additional scanned fingerprints.

Automated Fingerprint Identification Systems (AFIS)

the person who left it behind. Currently, chemicals and laser beams are used to lift latent prints from almost anything, including porous material like paper, clothing, and even snow.

An excellent example of the benefits of this new technique is the celebrated 1986–87 Los Angeles case in which a man with an ax attacked the Secretary of State of California in her home and robbed her of $400 to support his cocaine habit. He stuffed the money in an envelope and ran out of the house. A couple of blocks away he threw away the envelope, no doubt, realizing that it was addressed to the secretary. Several days later somebody found the envelope with the imprint of a bloody fingerprint and turned it over to the police. By using chemicals, Los Angeles police officers were able to lift the single fingerprint from the envelope, photograph and enlarge it, and feed it into the California Automated Fingerprint Identification System discussed later in this chapter. The system then identified the minutiae points, searched one of its databases for a match, and a few minutes later the computer came up with a possible suspect. A fingerprint technician compared the latent print with the print in the database and verified that it was a "hit." That is, the latent print was identified and matched to the fingerprint of 27-year-old Gregory Lee Moore, a parolee. A warrant was issued, and two days later with the assistance of a police dog the suspect was apprehended.

THE CALIFORNIA AUTOMATED IDENTIFICATION SYSTEM

Because the manual fingerprint matching and identifying process is slow and tedious, prototypes of computer-aided fingerprint matching and identifying systems were installed twenty years ago by the FBI and by the Canadian Mounted Police. A developing computer application called ALSM will provide an online searching and matching capability of latent fingerprints against AIS databases via a matching algorithm. A production mode in a high-tech Automated Fingerprint Information System (AFIS) is scheduled on the federal level. For years states were unhappy with the time factor in sending fingerprint cards to AIS—waiting to have them processed and to have the findings mailed back took several days. California law enforcement officials were especially unhappy.

The California Department of Justice (DOJ) has 7.5 million fingerprints on file (the largest fingerprint file in the United States after the FBI's in Washington, DC). The DOJ staff decided in the late 1970s that there was a dire need to have their own high-tech AFIS. Subsequently, in 1985—after comprehensive research and analysis—California's DOJ staff selected a fingerprint matching and identifying computer system, designed, developed, and manufactured by Nippon Electronic Corp. (NEC) of Japan (FIG. 4-4). In April 1985 the staff began the first phase of

The California Automated Identification System

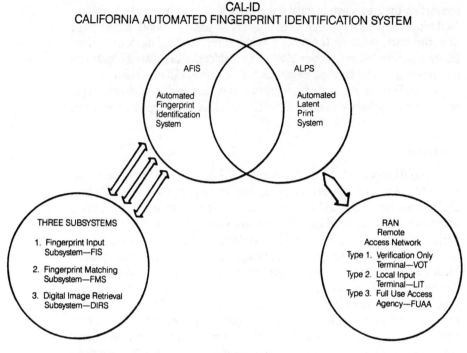

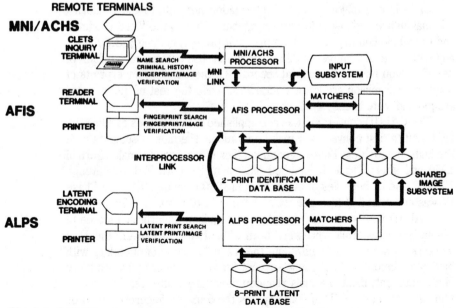

Fig. 4-4. CAL-ID automated fingerprint and subject identification system.

Automated Fingerprint Identification Systems (AFIS)

converting their massive manual fingerprint files to an automated system. As it often happens with such large projects, it wasn't smooth sailing right from the start. Actually, the project failed to receive funding twice before finally it succeeded in October 1985. The California Automated Identification System (CAL-ID) then began its highly successful operation.

CAL-ID is an automated fingerprint matching and identification system that is a nationwide and worldwide model for such high-tech system.

An Overview

CAL-ID, operated by the California DOJ and located in Sacramento, is one of the most sophisticated automated fingerprint matching and identifying systems in use today. What makes this system stand out among other existing automated identification systems is NEC's *relational* comparison technique. Most other AFIS systems' method for comparison is to check the minutiae in the form of ridge ending and bifurcation points. Such methods work well with clean prints. But latent and partial prints can be distorted, degrading the accuracy of the minutiae. The NEC system of CAL-ID uses for data the number of ridges between minutiae points, which is immune to distortion. Points are compared as to how many ridges are in between them. Moreover, in spite of the additional computations associated with handling the relational data, NEC matching processors each match at the rate of 1.34 milliseconds per print. This equals approximately 650 matches checked per second.

CAL-ID is a major source of information not only to the California criminal justice and law enforcement agencies, but to the Western states and the whole country. CAL-ID, a five-year project, costing $23.5 million and with an annual budget of $2 million, so far has automated 5 million of its 7.5 million manual fingerprint records. Of the 5 million fingerprints of subjects, 1.8 million are known offenders, while the rest of the subjects are job and state license applicants.

The CAL-ID conversion was accomplished in four phases to allow the DOJ staff to first convert and make operational the files of subjects with the highest activities. Phase I contained files of males and females born in 1960 and after; Phase II included files of males born in 1950 through 1959; Phase III held files of males born in 1940 through 1949; and Phase IV was comprised of files of females born in 1940 through 1959.

CAL-ID now stores and maintains 1.8 million fingerprint records of criminals in California who were born after 1940. Moreover, the DOJ workers do not intend to automate the manual records of offenders with birthdates before 1940 because, except for sex offenders who are more likely to repeat, most criminals abandon their career after reaching a certain age. Besides, the DOJ staff expects the 5 million fingerprint records in CAL-ID to grow to some 8 million within the next 5 years, if not sooner.

The California Automated Identification System

In addition to entering, matching, identifying, storing, and maintaining fingerprints of both felony and misdemeanor offenders, CAL-ID also stores fingerprints of various job and license applicants for a background check. These are the people who apply for a job with a law enforcement or criminal justice agency, or people who are being considered for a job that involves handling sensitive information or money. People who want to operate a liquor store, a cardroom, a day care center, security service, or any other business that requires a state license must have their fingerprints submitted to CAL-ID on a file card. In addition to verifying that the applicant does not have a criminal record in California, the applicant agency receives a response from the DOJ consistent with the civil rights of the applicant and the needs of the agency. In other words, the entire record is not returned routinely to the agency.

The completeness of the responses have been established by court order and introduced into law as a result of *Central Valley Chapter of the 7th Step Foundation vs. Evelle J. Younger*, Attorney General of the State of California, litigation filed in Alameda Superior Court in 1978.

The DOJ's CAL-ID operates according to the following rules concerning *retainability* and *nonretainability* of records:

1. A ten-print card is retainable if it provides a basis for a *criminal record* or *applicant record*.

    - *A criminal record* means the charge (offense) must be one that carries potential jail or prison sentence.
    - *An applicant record* means the application must be for licensing, certification, or specific employment where the state is required by law to provide identification services.

2. An infraction of a local ordinance or one that involves a potential fine is nonretainable.

    - If an offense is expressly *nonbookable*, then it is nonretainable. (Nonbookable means that no fingerprints are taken.)

Note: On the average, CAL-ID receives 2,500 applicants' and 2,500 criminals' fingerprint cards per day for processing.

CAL-ID's Configuration

CAL-ID, a totally integrated identification system, is composed of two databases, one multilevel network, and three subsystems. (See FIG. 4-1.)

CAL-ID's hardware configuration includes twenty-six matching NEC

Automated Fingerprint Identification Systems (AFIS)

mini computers that are connected to a large NEC mainframe. Each of the NEC matching processors cost the DOJ approximately $250,000. But CAL-ID's configuration allows the DOJ to process 4,000 ten-fingerprint inquiries and 280 latent fingerprint inquiries per day.

The following three types of machines make fingerprint matching possible in CAL-ID:

- *Fingerprint Readers.* These are analog-to-digital converter devices that transform an image of any sort into digital data, so that the computer system can process it.
- *Image Processor Computers.* These computers produce the images used in minutiae detection and verification from the initial grey-scale data.
- *Fingerprint Matching Processors.* These processors match the fingerprints that the previous machines converted into digital data.

CAL-ID uses some magnetic disks, but its primary media is optical disks. The minutiae data used in the matching process are stored on magnetic disks. However, for each minutiae record obtained from a fingerprint, a binary image of the ridge detail of the fingerprint is stored on optical disks. Each disk has a capacity of 180,000 fingerprint images. Optical disks are kept online to respond to image requests in less than 15 seconds.

CAL-ID's Two Identification Databases

The Automated Fingerprint Identification System (AFIS). AFIS stores the fingerprint ridge characteristics, that is, the minutiae from the thumbs of both criminals and applicants whose *rolled* fingerprint cards are on file, and who were born in 1940 and after. Besides the fingerprints of two thumbs, AFIS contains biographical information and the CII number (which is the same as the SID number) assigned to the subject's file by DOJ's Bureau of Criminal Identification (BCID). Interestingly, a CII number is assigned not only to criminals, but to employees of law enforcement and criminal justice agencies as well.

AFIS is used to conduct routine searches, including rolled fingerprint cards that are sent to DOJ for a *technical*, or routine, search. In 1987 routine searches were conducted on more than 550,000 fingerprint cards by AFIS, whose database contained more than five million records by December of that year.

AFIS is divided into three sections: Section I contains the thumb prints of felony offenders, Section II contains the thumb prints of misdemeanor offenders, and Section III contains the thumb prints of job and license applicants. Whenever an applicant is fingerprinted, or a suspect is

The California Automated Identification System

arrested and fingerprinted, that individual's tenprint card or source document is filed and his or her thumb print is entered into AFIS. If the arrested person is convicted, the minutiae data of eight fingers is entered in ALPS (the next database on the agenda), and the thumb prints become permanent records in AFIS. If the suspect is found innocent and released, his or her fingerprints are not entered into ALPS, the thumb prints are deleted from AFIS, and the fingerprint card is removed from the files.

When an inquiry with a fingerprint card comes in from a law enforcement or criminal justice agency to identify a particular person, first it goes for possible matching to the Automated Criminal History System (ACHS), a subsystem of Criminal Justice Information System (CJIS), another vital computer system operated by the DOJ. Although CJIS is a separate, stand-alone system, CAL-ID and CJIS do interact. (See chapter 5 for a thorough discussion of CJIS.) To be more precise, the inquiry goes to Master Name Index (MNI), a huge database of ACHS that contains more than 11 million names and biographical notations. If there is a hit on MNI, the inquiry goes to fingerprint verification, but it is not searched in CAL-ID. If there is no hit on MNI, the request is sent to CAL-ID's ALPS for search, verification, or matching. If ALPS is unable to come up with a hit, CAL-ID will so advise the requesting party.

The Automated Latent Print System (ALPS). ALPS stores the minutiae data from eight fingers of the 1.8 million individuals who have been arrested for felony crimes and who were born in or after 1940. The designers of CAL-ID system decided not to include the little fingers because the low hit rate on little fingers does not justify economically the minute information that the ridge characteristics of those fingers yield.

ALPS also is useful in investigative, *cold searches*. Cold searches include searches of individual, partial, and smudged latent fingerprints found by dust powder, chemicals, or laser, and lifted at the scene of a crime. Such fingerprints are matched against fingerprints in ALPS for possible hits. Actually, ALPS has the capability of taking a single latent print and through its *latent-cognizant* or *pattern recognition* technique run it through its database for possible matching. By December 1987 ALPS's database was storing more than one and a half million records.

CAL-ID's Multilevel Network

Remote Access Network (RAN). CAL-ID's Remote Access Network (RAN) provides law enforcement agencies the necessary equipment to access records directly in AFIS and ALPS. This capability allows local sheriffs and police officers who participate in RAN to identify or verify suspects on the terminal's screen in minutes. (See FIG. 4-5.)

Although technically there are two types of remote access devices

Automated Fingerprint Identification Systems (AFIS)

Fig. 4-5. CAL-ID's Remote Access Network.

installed in local law enforcement agencies that participate in CAL-ID's RAN, in actuality there are three types of RAN installations.

The Verification Only Terminal. The Verification Only Terminal (VOT) is an inexpensive remote access device. It is, however, limited to access CAL-ID only for verification purposes. VOT can retrieve only fingerprint images stored in AFIS or ALPS and display them on the terminal's screen, or print them on paper to identify a person in custody, or identify a person from a list of suspects who might have left a latent print at the scene of a crime. VOT cannot input minutiae data to conduct a fingerprint search and it cannot conduct a name and/or biographical search in MNI. In short, VOT is a very limited law enforcement tool.

As an option to VOT, the DOJ has been working on a facsimile-type of equipment to offer a reasonably priced better network device. The facsimile terminal and communication network, which will be available in the near future, is called Image Transmission Device (ITD). ITD will allow small agencies to transmit rolled fingerprint cards and latent print tracings to CAL-ID and local databases for searching. Although ITD will benefit small agencies that cannot afford the expensive LIT and the even more expensive FUAA (description of these networks follow), larger agencies also will increase their capability through ITD because they will be able to service distant substations.

In addition, the DOJ will make available an enhanced VOT, dubbed Point-of-Booking Terminal. This device will have the database search capability of the more expensive LIT, but not LIT's sophisticated features or its speed. Still, the enhanced VOT will be very useful at local agencies where arrested suspects are booked.

The Local Input Terminal. The Local Input Terminal (LIT) costs more than a VOT, but it has many more capabilities. The LIT provides some highly sophisticated functions for local law enforcement agencies. LIT allows the participating local police and sheriff's agencies to input minutiae data and search ALPS for persons not identified locally. LIT can retrieve and display fingerprint images from DIRS (described below) to verify fingerprint and latent prints; can confirm the identity of persons in custody, and/or list possible suspects leaving latent prints at the scene of crime and then identify the person through minutiae matching.

Note: The City of Los Angeles has its own FUAA, called *Local Automated Fingerprint Identification System* (LAFIS). However, it accesses CAL-ID through the Los Angeles County FUAA, and therefore, to the CAL-ID system it looks as if the City of Los Angeles would have an LIT.

The Full Use Access Agency. The Full Use Access Agency (FUAA) is the most expensive type of RAN. It is a small version of CAL-ID in Sacramento. FUAA sets up and maintains its own automated fingerprint identification databases of criminals and applicants for the city, county, or other limited geographical region. FUAA also supports a network that permits agencies in the vicinity with VOTs and LITs to access its databases.

The following California counties have FUAAs and LITs: San Francisco, Alameda/Contra Costa, Los Angeles, San Diego, San Bernardino/Riverside, and Orange.

Note: The California Department of Justice staff members are considering using electronic *inkless fingerprint* recordings. These are devices that record minutiae electronically by having an individual place his or her fingers on an electronic pad that reads the minutiae. It eliminates flaws that occur with the traditional ink-rolled fingerprints.

Automated Fingerprint Identification Systems (AFIS)

CAL-ID's Three Subsystems

Fingerprint Input Subsystem. This subsystem inspects the fingerprints, detects minutiae from the fingerprint image, and inputs descriptive information about the minutiae.

This subsystem consists of the following:

- The Fingerprint Reader (FR) examines fingerprint cards and generates minutiae data. It is comprised of a scanner that inspects fingerprint images from rolled fingerprint cards; an image processor that detects skeletal patterns from the fingerprint image; and a minutiae detector that captures minutiae from the skeletal patterns.
- The Image Scanner (IS) inputs tenprint and latent fingerprint cards rejected by FR.
- The Fingerprint Input Monitor (FIM) checks and corrects, if necessary, fingerprint image data inputs from FR, as well as descriptive information and display images retrieved from Digital Image Retrieval Subsystem (described later).
- The Magnetic Disk Unit stores the application software, and provides temporary files for fingerprint image and minutiae data.

Fingerprint Matching Subsystem. This subsystem compares entered fingerprints with fingerprints stored in the CAL-ID databases, and selects prints with a high degree of similarity to the *searchprint*.

This subsystem consists of the following:

- The Fingerprint Matching Processor (FMP), compares searchprints with fingerprints in the databases, and generates the candidate list.
- The Online Terminal (OT), which is essentially a work station (a FIM) attached to the Matching Subsystem (rather than to an I-Sub). However, it has no image capability, that is, it cannot display an image. It is used as a system monitor.
- Magnetic Disk Units in addition to the application and system software, are used to store the minutiae database. That is, the minutiae are only on magnetic disks. There are 86 365-megabyte disks online in CAL-ID.
- The Magnetic Tape Unit performs statistical management of system operations, and provides backup for fingerprint data.

Digital Image Retrieval Subsystem (DIRS). The DIRS allows the fingerprint technician to visually check, that is, to verify whether the searchprint actually corresponds to the fileprint.

The California Automated Identification System

This subsystem consists of the following:

- DIRS Controller, which controls all optical disks and communication with Input and Matching subsystems
- Optical Disk Unit, which stores the fingerprint image of the thumb, index, middle, and ring fingers, using binary images
- Magnetic Disk Unit, which stores programs and temporary image data
- Magnetic Tape Unit, which performs initial fingerprint loading, and provides backup for image files

DIRS is used in conjunction with AFIS and ALPS, and it automatically retrieves and stores fingerprint images contained in CAL-ID's two identification databases, and it displays those images on the computer terminal's screen.

It is DIRS that makes it possible for fingerprint experts to visually compare the fingerprints of the searched print to the fingerprints of the persons selected as possible matches by AFIS and ALPS without actually handling the fingerprint cards. DIRS also allows these fingerprint examiners to confirm or refute the identity of the person tentatively identified through MNI's name and biographical notations search.

DIRS's highly sophisticated comparison feature saves a tremendous amount of work and time for the experts, and expedites the probability of solving a particular case.

Finally, without DIRS it would not be practical for CAL-ID to have a multilevel, remote access network.

A CAL-ID-Like System in Europe

A CAL-ID counterpart has been installed recently in West Germany. It is called Bundeskriminalamt (BKA) and it is headquartered in Weisbaden. BKA is a national record and fingerprint depository, and it is linked to local, state, national, and continental law enforcement agencies through telecommunications systems. BKA is converting its 18 million tenprint cards to AFIS.

West German officials are quick to point out that, although BKA cost this country of 61.5 million people almost as much as CAL-ID, because of the use of BKA, law enforcement officers were able to solve 96 percent of serious offenses, including murder and rape. For example, the state police in North Rhein-West Phalia solved 400 serious crimes in the last three years through the almost instantaneous fingerprint identification ability of BKA. In general, however, BKA did not help in decreasing the rate of solved crimes in Germany—it remains about 50 percent. Nevertheless, just as CAL-ID, BKA is proving its worth every time a case is

Automated Fingerprint Identification Systems (AFIS)

solved or a criminal is caught through its effective automated fingerprint identification feature.

TWO PLANNED FUTURE ADDITIONS TO CAL-ID
Western Identification Network

The most ambitious addition to CAL-ID is planned in association with Western Identification Network (WIN), an organization incorporated under the laws of the State of Nevada in May, 1988. WIN is composed of member states and agencies within those member states. The twelve member states of WIN are: Alaska, Arizona, California, Colorado, Idaho, Montana, Nevada, New Mexico, Oregon, Utah, Washington, and Wyoming.

The primary object of WIN is to develop a cutting-edge automated fingerprint minutiae matching and processing system with networking capabilities to provide fast and accurate information to WIN member states and its agencies. This should help law enforcement officers to keep track of a large number of criminals, most of whom commit crimes in more than a single state or jurisdiction.

Another objective of WIN is to overcome the traditional reluctance of the staff of law enforcement agencies and departments in different states and even in the same state to share information. Of course, quite often this reluctance is based on budgetary reasons, because providing information to another agency might help solve a crime, but it adds nothing to the originating agency's crime solved record or image. Simply put, it will not help justify the originating agency's budget or its staff.

This project is much more than a future possibility. The system is ready for use. Moreover, both the Western States Attorneys General Association and the Western States Governors Association unanimously approved the concept. (See appendix A.)

An Overview. WIN will have the capability to perform technical searches against a Tenprint database; the capability to perform tenprint searches against a Latent database; and the capability to perform tenprint searches against an Unsolved Latent database. It will have the capability to verify fingerprint images—without referencing the cards in a manual file—to confirm results of a search, and it will have a data entry capability to set up and maintain the Tenprint, Latent, and Unsolved Latent databases. Although the databases will be located at the central site, all the remote sites will be able to conduct search and verification processes, as well as inquiries. Selected authorized remote sites will be able to add, change, or delete records in any of the databases. The system will be able to accept searches and inquiries from remote sites; route them to the appropriate processor, whether it's the Tenprint database, the Latent

Two Planned Future Additions to CAL-ID

database, or the Unsolved Latent database; and expeditiously communicate the response to the originator.

WIN's Configuration. The WIN system is much more than a *network*. WIN will have capabilities that are unknown in the existing networks.

Consider the following:

- Network Interfacing. The system will have an interface capability with other existing automated fingerprint identification systems whether of similar or dissimilar manufacturer. Specifically, WIN will be able to send or receive search and verification requests from other similar or dissimilar AFIS systems, and send or receive the results from the originator.
- Search Forwarding. The system, after a search at WIN's central site, will have the capability to forward a search and verification to another AFIS—even of a dissimilar vendor—if the originator so requests.
- Image Processing and Minutiae Detection. WIN's electronic interface network will have the capability to transmit and receive demographic data, plus 20 pixel[1] per millimeter scan of the fingerprint ridge detail for each finger for accurate image processing and minutiae detection.
- Point-to-Point Electronic Mail Messages. For security reasons, WIN will have a point-to-point message transmission for the work stations within the network by using electronic mail.
- Broadcasting. The system will be able to broadcast to the remote sites about a scheduled unavailability of the system, or any other information vital to the remote sites.

The second planned addition to CAL-ID is a DNA database.

The DNA Database. Although "the world's first automated database containing DNA identification" that California State Attorney General John Van de Kamp advocates is still some five years away, DNA is too important a definitive identification technique in fighting crime not to be discussed in relation to CAL-ID.

To start with, DNA or deoxyribonucleic acid, the well-known genetic code, was discovered in the 1960s. A DNA molecule—whether it be a drop of blood, a trace of semen or saliva, a fragment of skin, or a hair root—contains an individual's entire biological blueprint in chemical codes. To be more precise, a single cell contains the DNA code to a person's sex, race, bone structure, skin and hair color, blood type, and the

---

[1] *Pixel* refers to a picture element. A pixel is a small rectangular division of the VDT or video display screen. The smaller the rectangular, the sharper the picture. The higher the resolution, the more rectangulars.

Automated Fingerprint Identification Systems (AFIS)

like, and the DNA code can be matched to any other cell from the same individual. Moreover, except for identical twins, the odds against two persons having exactly the same DNA patterns are about 30 billion to 1.

At the beginning of 1988, two molecular biologists at the Massachusetts Institute of Technology (MIT) discovered a second genetic code and its functions in all living cells alongside DNA. Eventually, this scientific breakthrough should further enhance DNA's role as a powerful police tool.

To effect a DNA code, forensic scientists chemically analyze the sample human tissue in certain sequences known as the *DNA probes*. The result looks like a bar code or Universal Product Code (UPC) used on grocery store items.

This technique provides tremendous potential aid in criminal investigations where there are no fingerprints left at the scene of crimes. A single strand of hair left at the scene of a crime can, through the DNA technique, become an undeniable proof linking a suspect to a crime.

The interest is so great in DNA technology that the FBI assigned a task force to explore wider applications of this new technology. The California DOJ has set up a six-member advisory board consisting of police chiefs, sheriffs, district attorneys, and an FBI representative to supervise the planned DNA database program. However, the American Civil Liberties Union (ACLU) has a lot of reservations. ACLU members voiced concern as to the possible misuse of this technique and the privacy of the individual involved in a DNA testing. There are still some problems to be worked out before the DNA database can be created. These problems include regulations for the collection, storage, standard quality-control rules for analyzing DNA samples, and court acceptance. Yet, California and Colorado have already instituted a rule whereby convicted sex offenders are required to give DNA samples. The sample analyses are kept on file in case the offenders commit another crime.

In England DNA analysis has been used for many years by the British Home Office in immigration and paternity cases. However, it was not until September 1987 when forensic scientists matched the DNA genetic structure of the saliva of a suspect in the rape and murder case of two 15-year-old girls with semen found in the victims that the police used this technique in a homicide. Moreover, because of the DNA test, a 17-year-old youth who first had been charged with the killings was released, and a 35-year-old man, who confessed after being confronted with the result of his DNA test, was convicted and sentenced to life in prison.

The very first criminal case in the United States in which a person's conviction was based primarily on a DNA test happened in Orlando, Florida. The case concerned a 24-year-old man who was arrested in the spring of 1987 and charged with two in a series of nearly two dozen rapes in the Orlando area in 1986. Because the rapist always covered his victim's face and did not leave any fingerprints behind, the prosecutors were

Two Planned Future Additions to CAL-ID

concerned about a possible acquittal. A DNA test compared the man's blood to semen found in the victims. The samples matched and the man was convicted, and sent to prison.

Of course, forensic science and forensic evidence—particularly in the fingerprint, drugs, and firearms areas—have been around for decades. In fact, many criminologists felt that "forensic sciences are overburdened and underutilized." Actually, until the recent breakthrough by scientists in the DNA genetic code, law enforcement officers considered forensic evidence pertaining to blood, semen, hair, and skin tissues, as weak, inconclusive evidence.

But now, because it has been conclusively proven that DNA tests can be conducted effectively up to five years on dried blood and saliva samples, and up to 3 years on dried semen, prosecutors both in this country and in England are quite enthusiastic about "finally having a foolproof test to use in criminal cases." This enthusiasm is, however, dampened by the fact that the average cost per case is $1,000.

5

Criminal Justice Information Systems and Law Enforcement Telecommunications Systems

CRIMINAL JUSTICE INFORMATION SYSTEMS

By now almost all 50 states have their own automated CJIS. They might have different names and their system might contain health and welfare records, and records concerning juvenile and adult arrests, misdemeanors, and traffic accidents, in addition to criminal history and fingerprint records but basically they are the same type of system.

A CJIS—whether in Ohio or Hawaii—is a computerized criminal justice information system that is a counterpart of FBI's NCIC in Washington, and is maintained by the DOJ in each state. It is available to authorized local, state, and federal law enforcement and criminal justice agencies via any of the three law enforcement telecommunication systems. (Refer to the descriptions of CLETS, NLETS, and INLETS later in this chapter.) Generally, a CJIS offers a much wider range of information and more precise inquiry search parameters than NCIC because of the nationwide scope of NCIC. Large states such as California, Illinois, Ohio, Texas, and New York, have, in addition to a state-run CJIS, regional automated police information systems for more local details.

Some CJISs across the country are very efficient in providing fast, accurate information to their local and state law enforcement agencies;

some could be improved. It is essential to understand that the primary role of any criminal justice information system is to make available to authorized law enforcement officers up-to-date, reliable information. Such information is necessary to identify, apprehend, and clear suspects, match found or pawned property with stolen property, determine whether there is a warrant on the suspect, or if the suspect has a prior criminal record. In certain situations the information can save an officer's life. In fact, what makes this system such a powerful tool for the patrol officer is that the information in the CJIS databases can be accessed in less than a minute via NLETS and a Mobile Digital Terminal (MDT), Message Switching Computer (MSC), or Computer Aided Dispatch (CAD) in the officer's patrol car.

Because the California CJIS, located in Sacramento and managed by the California DOJ, is one of the most sophisticated and comprehensive law enforcement information systems in the country, it lends itself well as an example of an effective automated criminal justice system.

AN OVERVIEW OF THE CALIFORNIA CRIMINAL JUSTICE INFORMATION SYSTEM

The California CJIS is a cooperative endeavor between state and local agencies. The California DOJ maintains the CJIS at its main facility in Sacramento. Individual California law enforcement and criminal justice agencies, however, are responsible for the records they input to CJIS. Agencies that enter and update records are responsible for the accuracy and integrity of those records. To ensure that the records are accurate and that the data integrity within the CJIS databases are protected, the users must adhere to the strict policies established by the DOJ.

CONFIGURATION OF CJIS

CJIS consists of seven databases and one subsystem, and its retrieval and update capabilities are online. Its hardware consists of a Sperry mainframe containing a four-megaword CPU and a System Transition Unit that makes partitioning and reconfiguration possible. CJIS hardware also includes a special system console and a General Communications Subsystem that can handle line speeds from 110 baud to 56,000 bits per second.

A description of CJIS databases and its subsystem follows.

THE SEVEN MAJOR DATABASES OF CJIS
Wanted Persons System

The Wanted Persons System (WPS) database contains profiles of wanted persons, information on warrants issued on prison escapees,

The Seven Major Databases of CJIS

information on people who failed to respond to a subpoena, or offenders who are known to be armed and dangerous. This database maintains and stores 500,000 records.

Information on wanted persons is also available to authorized California law enforcement officers from NCIC. Furthermore, the California Department of Motor Vehicles maintains some warrant information on its Driver License databases that might assist police officers.

The WPS database contains the following details about each offender:

- Name (NAM)
- Date of birth (DOB)
- Also known as (AKA)
- Date of Warrant (DOW)
- Warrant number (WAR)
- Extradition information (EXT)
- Type of warrant (TOW)
- Sex (SEX)
- Race (RACE)
- Weight (WGT)
- Scars, marks, and tattoos (SMT)
- Date of locate (DOL)
- Date of purge (DOP)
- CII number (CII)
- NCIC number (NIC)
- Originating agency identifier (ORI)
- Originating agency case number (OCA)
- Offense Code (OFF)
- Caution statement (CAU)

Stolen Vehicle System

The Stolen Vehicle System (SVS) database includes information about stolen and felony vehicles that can be traced by the vehicle identification number (VIN), engine ID, or license plate. The database maintains and stores more than 620,000 records. If a patrol officer wants to find out if a vehicle or vehicle license plate is on the wanted list, he can get instantaneous information from the SVS database. More specifically, if the officer needs to find out if a vehicle or license plate is wanted by a criminal justice agency, he should access SVS and NCIC. If the officer needs to know who is the owner of the vehicle, he should access the State Department of Motor Vehicles (DMV).

The SVS database contains the following details:

- Originating agency identifier (ORI)
- Originating agency case number (OCA)

- Date of transaction (DOT)
- Vehicle identification number (VIN)
- License plate number (LIC)
- Vehicle make (VMA)
- Vehicle model (VMO)
- Vehicle style (VST)
- Vehicle year (VYR)
- Owner applied number (OAN)
- Date of locate (DOL)
- File control number (FCN)
- NCIC number (NCIC)
- Locating agency case number (LAC)
- Recovering agency identifier (RAI)
- Locate delete (LOC)
- Reason for cancellation (REASON)

Information contained in Wanted Persons and Stolen Vehicle databases is the most crucial to patrol officers. The data provided can determine whether the officer should be cautious when approaching a vehicle stopped for a minor traffic violation.

Automated Firearms System

The Automated Firearms System (AFS) database contains information on registered firearms, as well as stolen and recovered firearms. The database maintains and stores more than six million records. Information regarding stolen and recovered firearms that is input into AFS is forwarded automatically to NCIC's Stolen and Recovered Firearms database.

Note: According to the penal code of many states, it is mandatory for law enforcement agency officers to enter stolen, lost, found, recovered, or under observation property into the appropriate automated database. Many states have a penal code that mandates that the attorney general file copies of applications for licenses to carry concealed weapons, and file copies of dealers' records of sales of revolvers or pistols, as well as reports of stolen, lost, found, or pawned property anywhere in the state. Because of these mandates, all records submitted to AFS must be based on a master case record by the originating agency. The master case records must be maintained by the originating agency.

This database contains the following details:

- Name (NAM)
- Date of birth (DOB)

The Seven Major Databases of CJIS

- Social security number (SOC)
- Type of firearm (TYP)
- Make (manufacturer's code) (MAK)
- Serial number (SER)
- Originating agency identification (ORI)
- Operator's license number (OLN)
- Originating agency case number (OCA)
- Locating agency case number (LAC)
- CII number (CII)
- Date of locate (DOL)
- Date of transaction (DOT)
- Address of the person in the record (ADR)
- City/County (CCC)
- Category of the firearm (CAT)
- Caliber (size of the bullet) (CAL)

Automated Boat System

The Automated Boat System (ABS) database is the California counterpart of NCIC's Stolen and Recovered Boats and Marine Equipment database. The California Vehicle Code (Section 10551) directs law enforcement officers to input to ABS any reliable report they receive about stolen or recovered boats.

This database contains the following information:

- Boat hull number (BHN)
- Boat color (BCO)
- Boat length (BLE)
- Boat make (BMA)
- Brand (brand name of boat part) (BRA)
- Boat type (BTY)
- Boat model year (BYR)
- Date of transaction (DOT)
- Engine number (ENG)
- File control number (FCN)
- Originating agency identifier (ORI)
- Originating agency case number (OCA)
- NCIC number (NIC)
- Owner applied number (OAN)
- Recovery agency identifier (RAI)
- Registration number (REG)
- Serial number (SER)
- Locating agency case number (LAC)

- Locate delete (LOC)
- Date of locate (DOL)
- Date of clear (DOC)
- Reason for cancellation (REASON)
- Caution code (CAU)

Automated Property/Stolen Bicycle System

The Automated Property/Stolen Bicycle database maintains and stores serial numbers and other data of stolen, lost, found, or pawned items and bicycles. It contains almost one million records.

Although NCIC also maintains a Stolen and Recovered Articles database, most CJIS databases around the country contain much more detail about stolen items, such as credit cards, bicycles, computers, radios, cameras, tools, than its counterpart in Washington, D.C.

This database contains the following details:

- Article (type of article) (ART)
- Brand (brand name) (BRA)
- Category (CAT)
- Date of transaction (DOT)
- Originating agency identifier (ORI)
- Originating agency case number (OCA)
- Owner applied number (OAN)
- NCIC number (NIC)
- Serial number (SER)
- Model number (MOD)
- Name (NAM)
- Value (VAL)
- File control number (FCN)
- Locating agency case number (LAC)
- Date of locate (DOL)
- Miscellaneous information (MIS)

Automated Criminal Intelligence Index/Western States Information Network

This database contains highly confidential information. It can be accessed only by the Bureau of Organized Crime and Criminal Intelligence (BOCCI). There are approximately 40,000 records maintained and stored in this database.

Adult Criminal Justice Statistical System

The Adult Criminal Justice Statistical System (ACJSS) database maintains statistical information on adult criminals.

AUTOMATED CRIMINAL HISTORY SYSTEM: A SUBSYSTEM OF CJIS

The Automated Criminal History System (ACHS) consists of several databases—including the huge Master Name Index (MNI)—and several indices. The master database of ACHS contains comprehensive information on persons within the state of California who have been arrested and fingerprinted for a serious crime such as felony, murder, or robbery. It also includes the nature of the crime and the disposition of the case, including details as to the name of the prison, if the person was convicted and the status of the person's probation/parole.

The database, which consists of 8.5 million records, maintains the following information:

- Name (NAM)
- Also known as (AKA)
- Date of birth (DOB)
- Date arrested (DAR)
- Crime (CRI)
- Originating agency identifier (ORI)
- Originating agency case number (OAC)
- Court case number (CCN)
- Disposition of the case (DOC)
- Criminal Identification and Information number (CII)
- Probation summary (PRS)
- Parole summary (PAS)
- Comments (COM)
- CAL-ID fingerprint classification (CAL)
- NCIC fingerprint classification (NIC)

ACHS serves the following user communities within the criminal justice community:

- Police and sheriff departments
- California Highway Patrol
- Prosecutors

Criminal Justice Information/Law Enforcement Telecommunication Systems

- Parole and probation officers
- Municipal and superior courts
- Correctional facilities
- City/county/district attorneys

ACHS serves the following user communities within the division of law enforcement:

- Bureau of Criminal Identification (BCID)
- Bureau of Criminal Statistics/Special Services (BCS/SS)
- Bureau of Organized Crime and Criminal Intelligence (BOCCI)
- Western States Information Network (WSIN)
- Bureau of Investigation (BI)
- Bureau of Narcotics Enforcement (BNE)

ACHS is used to provide criminal history information to authorized noncriminal justice agencies for licensing and employment.

ACHS also provides support to FBI and nearly every other state and local criminal justice agencies via Triple I.

Master Name Index

The MNI, a database of ACHS, is one of the largest and most important components of CJIS. MNI database, containing more than eleven million records, maintains and stores the name, known aliases, date of birth, and physical description of all persons who have a criminal or an applicant record on file at DOJ. Any offender who has his or her fingerprints in the ALPS and/or AFIS database of CAL-ID, or who has his or her record in the ACHS database, is included in MNI. In addition, any person who applies for a license to operate a specific business, or who applies for a job that requires the individual to be fingerprinted, and whose fingerprints and personal information are on the disks of AFIS, is included in MNI. Such jobs can be a security officer, bank teller, government or defense industry programmer, or analyst. The specific business can range from a daycare center or a nursing home to a liquor store or a gambling casino.

MNI is essential to the efficient operations of CAL-ID. Specifically, when an inquiry about a fingerprint card is submitted by a law enforcement officer for identification, it goes directly to MNI. If there is a match on MNI, the card goes to fingerprint verification without involving CAL-ID. This detour to MNI saves CAL-ID a tremendous amount of processing, time, and effort. When all the data is gathered about the suspect, a response is sent to the originating agency. When there is no match on MNI the inquiry is directed to CAL-ID's ALPS database for search and

Automated Criminal History System: A Subsystem of CJIS

matching. If ALPS is not able to come up with a match CAL-ID will send a response to the requesting agency.

Following are some of the details that are in this online database:

- CII number (CII)
- Name (NAM)
- Date of birth (DOB)
- Sex (SEX)
- Race (RACE)
- Height (HGT)
- Weight (WGT)
- Eye color (EYE)
- Hair color (HAIR)
- Place of birth (POB)
- Social security number (SOC)
- California Driver's License number (CDL)
- Scars/marks/tattoos (SMT)
- Out of state driver's license number (OLN)
- Occupation(s) (OCC)

Western States Information Network (WSIN) and Organized Crime Database

These two CJIS-connected computer systems are unique in many respects. They are the most secure of all the computer systems that are located at the California DOJ in Sacramento; they do not go through CLETS; they cannot be accessed from field offices; and they are connected directly to CJIS.

Although both WSIN and the Organized Crime Unit use the CJIS operating system and its application software, they are completely independent of each other. They each have the CJIS applications modified to respond to their unique needs. The hardware for both of these systems is the mainframe, Unisys 1100 Model 90.

WSIN. WSIN was established February 27, 1981. It fills a much needed information computer network for the narcotic intelligence needs of law enforcement agencies in five states—Alaska, California, Hawaii, Oregon, and Washington. The host agency for WSIN is the California DOJ, and all the agency staff people have to phone their requests for information to the host agency.

WSIN was designed to provide this service because exchange of information on the multijurisdictional scope of narcotic trafficking is an important factor in successful narcotic enforcement. WSIN is a central repository of information on narcotics traffickers; an analytical support service for identifying narcotic trafficking organizations; and a coordinator of investigations among jurisdictions. All of this service is provided solely through the host agency.

Only officers designated by their agency as primary liaison officers or alternate liaison officers can ask WSIN for information via telephone because the security of such information is essential. Access to the WSIN-maintained Automated Criminal Intelligence Index (ACII) database is limited to specified WSIN personnel. This measure further assures tight security.

The data entered into the ACII database is submitted by member agencies on WSIN format cards. The information pertains to narcotic subjects, aircraft, vessels, and illegal drug laboratories.

The analytical services provided by WSIN include: link analysis, telephone toll analysis, visual investigative analysis, and event flow charts. In addition, WSIN analysts are involved in research projects, such as use of drug-detecting canines, narcotic involvement by outlaw motorcycle gangs, organized crime's involvement in drugs, drug smuggling from South America, narcotic-related homicides, and so on.

The features and functions of the Organized Crime database are similar to WSIN. The operations and application software is tailored for its unique needs and requirements.

LAW ENFORCEMENT TELECOMMUNICATION SYSTEMS

Every one of the three telecommunication systems—NLETS, INLETS, and CLETS—used in this country by criminal justice and law enforcement agencies is a high-speed message switching system enabling agencies across and beyond the country to communicate.

NLETS

NLETS, based in Phoenix, Arizona, is an administrative network. It allows law enforcement agency officers in all fifty states to access NCIC records in Washington, D.C., for information on wanted or missing persons, criminal history, stolen/felony vehicles, stolen firearms, and stolen property. Moreover, this high-speed message switching system also provides agency staff members across the country an efficient tool to communicate with each other. NLETS makes it possible to transmit and receive point-to-point messages, as well as send a message through the multiple address feature, to up to six law enforcement agencies.

INLETS

INLETS, based in Washington, D.C., at the FBI headquarters, is used to communicate with INTERPOL in London, as well as with other overseas law enforcement agencies.

CLETS

CLETS is based at the California DOJ headquarters in Sacramento, and was created by a legislative act in 1965. It has been in operation since April, 1970. CLETS, similar to CJIS, is a cooperative effort of the California DOJ and local law enforcement agencies. DOJ provides the hardware, the circuitry to one point in each county, and the staff to run the switching center at its headquarters. Local agencies provide the circuitry and equipment that link the agency to its county terminal point.

The fact is that without CLETS, law enforcement agencies would not be able to access CJIS, utilize CAL-ID, or reach NCIC for essential data. If, for example, an officer in the field has a mobile data terminal (MDT) in his patrol car, he can access CJIS or CAL-ID directly through CLETS without going through the dispatcher, saving precious time.

An officer in California can get information from that state's CJIS or DMV through CLETS. The officer also can inquire into Triple I, AIS, or any of the twelve NCIC databases, or the ACHS of the State of Oregon by accessing CLETS. If the inquiry is directed to an out-of-state criminal justice information system, CLETS, after it validates the message, assigns a number to the message, and determines the correct routing. CLETS reformats the message and transmits it through NLETS to its destination.

The records in CJIS are updated through CLETS by the staff of more than 650 local criminal justice and law enforcement agencies. Because of the pertinence of privacy and data integrity issues, the agency workers are responsible for relevance of the data they enter. That is, the DOJ rules and regulations in regard to accessing and updating data in CJIS are strictly observed by the agencies.

Finally, CLETS has the capability to switch 17,000 messages per hour, and provides service 24 hours a day, seven days a week. Its hardware configuration consists of two Sperry 90/80 processors and seven distributed communications processors that work in conjunction with a multichannel communications processor to verify messages before going to the CPU.

6

Intellect Investigations System, United Crime Alert Network, Computer-Aided Dispatch, and Other Software Applications

Criminal justice and law enforcement agencies are information processing organizations. Consequently, any media, such as computer systems, that eliminate tedious and time-consuming tasks and expedite police work is a welcome help.

Following is a sampling of the varied software applications designed for and used almost exclusively by law enforcement agencies.

INTELLECT INVESTIGATIONS SYSTEM[1]

Intellect Investigations System is unique among the hundreds, if not thousands, of computer software programs designed specially for law enforcement professionals who are not computer literate. For one thing, it is an artificial intelligence-based expert system. Secondly, the software

---

[1] Through the courtesy of Artificial Intelligence Corp., 100 Fifth Ave., Waltham, MA, 02254-9156

Intellect Investigations System

program is a powerful interactive tool that enables nontechnical police and sheriff staff to develop programs that respond to their needs by using conversational English.

Before describing Intellect Investigations System in detail, a nontechnical discussion of *artificial intelligence (AI)* and *expert systems* is in order.

AI, a branch of computer science, is a field of study generally concerned with designing computer systems that emulate human thinking. Research in AI resulted in robotics, better understanding of cognitive processes as developed in cognitive science, that is, knowledge representation, and expert systems, among many other applications.

Cognitive science is an interdisciplinary, comparatively new branch of behavioral science that deals with human/computer interaction, analysis of human behavior, pattern recognition, and cognitive style. Incidentally, the last two features are used extensively by the FBI in their criminal profiling technique.

AI applications' main characteristic is judgment, a feature that separates applications—such as expert systems—from the conventional computer applications. Because judgment is central in any law enforcement investigation, expert systems are making an inroad in automated crime information systems. Actually, expert systems are an economically and operationally viable product of AI that utilizes the knowledge and inference areas of AI to be able to come up with a judgment.

All these features make Intellect Investigations System a powerful tool for nontechnical law enforcement staff. Because of the simple, conversational English language provided by Intellect, the staff can easily develop programs tailor-made for their needs. End users who need fast access to information can retrieve, add, change, or delete data in the Intellect database without first learning a complex programming language.

Configuration of Intellect Investigations System

Intellect Investigations System, as most expert systems, starts with a shell into which an expert supplies basic knowledge (of a specific field) and what computer scientists call *inference*. Inference is decision rules or rules of thumb that an expert employs to make a decision. In other words, the expert system makes a determination by means of knowledge and *heuristics*, a method of problem solving through trial and error. Thus, a database is built on basic knowledge, rules of thumb, and fundamental data.

Method of Operation

When Intellect Investigations System receives a request (in simple English), it breaks apart the inquiry to determine what information is

Intellect Investigations System[1]

being requested. Then it identifies the fields in its database that contain the targeted information. Next, it determines if other fields, in addition to those requested, might be useful to the requestor for better interpretation of results. Intellect actually asks the user if any additional information would help in establishing the identity of the suspect, for example, to solve the problem.

Note: A user can search for the identity of a suspect by using a general physical description, modus operandi, aliases or nicknames, types of crime, and prison and parole terms.

This expert system is able to perform these tasks by referencing its dictionary. When an expert system—in this instance Intellect Investigations System—is implemented at any criminal justice or law enforcement agency, its dictionary or shell contains only a small vocabulary of root words. These root words are verbs, nouns, and pronouns common to most applications, such as reports, sorts, files, and records. Next, data about the particular application is entered by the user (in this case criminal justice or law enforcement staff) with the assistance of a systems analyst.

Definitions of all data fields are created by the user and stored with synonyms, abbreviations, valid values, and other descriptive information. The dictionary is enhanced continuously and expanded by defining new terms and concepts based on those already defined.

The Sacramento County Sheriff's Department developed and implemented an Intellect Investigations System in six months with the assistance of one detective and one systems analyst from the county's computer center.

Another detective at the same facility has been working for many months on a string of burglaries. He decided to try to identify a suspect via the department's Intellect Investigations System. Because witnesses described the burglar as "tall, short, white, hispanic, and in his thirties, forties, fifties," the detective thought that the person might be an aging criminal out on parole.

Consequently, the detective asked the intellect system to "list all white males between the ages of 45 and 50, height between 5'6" and 6', weight between 180 and 200 pounds, that have been on parole for less than a year and have previous convictions for burglary."

The system returned one (instead of the usual five or six) match from some 900,000 other known offenders. The system also provided additional information on the suspect's drug habits.

Based on this information, the detective got the file photograph of the suspect, and the witnesses verified the match by the file photo. The suspect was located and arrested.

Intellect Investigations System

UNITED CRIME ALERT NETWORK[2]

United Crime Alert Network (UCAN), a cooperative effort between law enforcement agencies and the business community, is a low-cost, online crime alert software application that protects the business community, the retailers in particular. This is done by local law enforcement agencies communicating directly to businesses the most recent data on local on-going criminal activities that might affect the business community.

Configuration of UCAN

This software package consists of local law enforcement agencies sending their latest list of stolen/counterfeit/lost credit cards, and stolen and worthless checks, and information about fraud and robbery suspects from their database via a modem/telephone to a network of local merchants who are subscribers of UCAN. These business people must have a *dumb terminal* and a modem/telephone to receive the police communications. Contrary to *smart terminals*, which can be employed to access records and to add, change, or delete data from the database of a computer to which it is connected, dumb terminals can be used only to retrieve and display information on the screen.

Method of Operation

When a sales person of a local business receives a check or credit card, he presses one key on the store or restaurant's terminal and checks the up-to-the-minute crime data on the screen. The list provides an alphabetical name list for the previous 90 days and includes input from the city police, county sheriff, and officials from surrounding counties. If the sales person finds a match, he notifies the manager or owner for verification. The manager uses the code given next to the match in the list, and gets specific details from UCAN's stolen/worthless checks or lost/stolen counterfeit credit cards file.

If the sales person's match is verified, the manager follows the particular businesses' usual procedure in such cases.

This crime alert software costs less than $600 for installation and setup, plus $75 for phone/modem installation. In addition, there is a monthly charge for the use of the protection package.

---

[2]Through the courtesy of United Crime Alert Network, 23701 Mariner Dr., Suite 198, Laguna Niguel, CA 92677.

LANDTRAK[3]

LandTrak, in the forefront of graphics software applications, is a geo-based mapping and crime information analysis system. It is useful because it enables police and sheriff's departments to accurately track crime activities, analyze the effectiveness of vehicle location and patrol deployment strategies, provide crime and traffic exception reports, and identify the shortest path to crime locations.

Configuration of LandTrak

LandTrak is designed to run on the existing databases of large computer systems. In addition, there is a streamlined version of LandTrak—targeted for smaller police departments with tight budgets—that runs on microcomputers such as the IBM PC and all IBM-compatible personal computers.

To use LandTrak, the PC needs to have 640K random access memory (RAM), 10M hard disk storage, 2.0 or later version of PC/MSDOS, and monochrome adapter and monitor. For graphics accessories, Land-Trak requires a high resolution graphics card and color graphics monitor, Summagraphics Bit Pad/One or Microsoft Mouse, and a Hewlett-Packard Laser Jet +, or a Quadrum Quadjet Graphics Printer, or a similar printer.

Method of Operation

LandTrak stands out among geographic mapping systems because it can provide not only a map, but crime analysis as well. In addition, it is both user friendly and user definable. That is, law enforcement agency staff can tailor LandTrak for their own particular crime categories.

COMPUTER-AIDED DISPATCHING

Computer-Aided Dispatching (CAD) is an onboard software application that provides an automated entry and dispatch of police calls through the mobile computer terminal in the patrol car. CAD validates the location of calls via geo-base indexing; it maintains the status of units; it enables digital dispatching, that is, it provides message transmission from the law enforcement base to mobile computer terminal and from mobile data terminal to base; and it can generate status reports.

---

[3]Through the courtesy of Criterion, Inc., 13140 Coit Rd., Suite 318, Dallas, TX 75240.

Intellect Investigations System

Configuration of CAD

Most CAD applications are designed to be used on microcomputers that are connected to mini or large computers located either at the local police agency or at the city or county data processing center. CAD applications use local area networks for getting and sending information.

Method of Operation

When using CAD the police officer in the patrol car presses a key to get information, and hits another key to send information. If the officer needs to access NCIC in Washington or CJIS in his own state for information on a possible stolen car, outstanding warrants, or wanted person, he can do so via CLETS (if he's in California) or NLETS (if he's in any other state) without losing time having to go through the agency's dispatcher.

There are many CAD applications on the market.

POLICE-TRAK[4]

POLICE-TRAK is a microcomputer-based comprehensive law enforcement records management application. It consists of arrest files, property room records, name files, warrant files, uniform crime reporting, parking/traffic tickets, registration files, stolen property files, as well as budget files, case load management, internal affairs activity, and even a geo-based emergency locator.

The same vendor (Institute of Police Technology and Management) offers an application similar to POLICE-TRAK called POLICE COMPUTER SYSTEM. The only difference is that the latter is specifically designed for stand-alone microcomputers, such as the IBM PC or an IBM clone.

Configuration of POLICE-TRAK

POLICE-TRAK runs on a microcomputer-based local area network. It consists of a 20M hard disk and 640K memory server unit and as many terminals as necessary, all connected in a local area network.

Method of Operation

To use POLICE-TRAK the law enforcement officer accesses needed information by pressing certain keys on his terminal. And if he wants a hard copy of the information, he can easily and quickly print it out on the agency's printer.

---

[4]Through the courtesy of Institute of Police Technology and Management, University of Florida, 4567 St. Johns Bluff Road, So., Jacksonville, FL 32216.

RECORDS MANAGEMENT AND CRIME ANALYSIS SYSTEM[5]

The Records Management and Crime Analysis System consists of a name and location index, traffic analysis, management (processing) of criminal investigation, crime analysis, arrests, booking gang files, juvenile MO (modus operandi), detective case control, case tracking, adhoc reports, etc.

Configuration of Records Management and Crime Analysis System

The application can run on a microcomputer, mini, or large computer, as well as in a micro environment. It can also operate within a local area network (LAN).

Method of Operation

The use of this application is identical to POLICE-TRAK.

The official recording of the name, photograph, and fingerprints of a suspect, along with the offense charged, and the name of the officer who made the arrest.

FLEET MANAGEMENT SYSTEM (WHEELS)[6]

This law enforcement/public safety application consists of records of vehicle acquisition dates, records of fuel oil consumption and mileage during each period, records of types of maintenance performed and vehicle downtime hours, records of preventative maintenance verification and vehicle ID, and report generation.

Configuration of WHEELS

This application can run on micro-, mini-, or mainframe (large) computers, with or without local area network.

---

[5]Through the courtesy of Atkinson System Technologies, P.O. Box 1168, Sacramento, CA 95806.

[6]Through the courtesy of Cisco, Inc., 8018 Jumper Mall, Suite 241, Pasadena, Maryland 21122.

Intellect Investigations System

AUTOMATIC LOCATING VEHICLE SYSTEM[7]

The Automatic Locating Vehicle System (ALVS) is a real-time geo-based fleet management application that has the capability to interface with existing CAD systems; provide automated mapping; assist in contingency planning; and generate a vehicle activity history and scheduled and adhoc reports.

Configuration of ALVS

This customized application can run on stand-alone microcomputers and/or local area networks.

COMPUTER-AIDED MANAGEMENT OF EMERGENCY OP (CAMEO)[8]

Computer-Aided Management of Emergency Op (CAMEO) was designed to respond to chemical and hazardous material emergencies. Its modules consist of a large chemical database (names and definitions of 2,700 chemicals); a code breaker, i.e., it has a synonym chemical name search capability; a contingency planning feature; an air model, that is, an area location of hazardous atmospheres (ALOHA); a Station for Atmospheric Monitoring (SAM); and more.

Configuration of CAMEO

This is a MacIntosh-based application that is in the public domain.

CITYPOOL[9]

CITYPOOL is an effective and utilitarian municipal law enforcement application. It provides local law enforcement agencies with criminal history information, inquiry by name, aka (also known as), address, case/docket number, incident report, officer activity by shift, crime analysis, warrant information, case reporting by United Crime Reports (UCR) and/or internal PD offense codes.

---

[7]Through the courtesy of NAV-COM Inc., P.O. Box 650, Deer Park, NY 11729.

[8]For further information of how this application matches the chemical to a chemical in the database to provide toxic information, please call the agency who designed it—NOAA/WASC, U.S. Department of Commerce-OAD HAZM, 7600 Sand Point Way Northeast, Seattle, WA 98115.

[9]Through the courtesy of Designer Software Consultant, Inc., 4815-B Odessa Ave., Fort Worth, TX 76133.

Configuration of CITYPOOL

This application can run on mini or microcomputers and LANs, or even as a stand-alone system. It has a nonhardware dependent password security capability.

It's worth a mention of two of the better known applications among the dozens of computer programs that have sprung up in police departments across the country.

One of these applications is the New Orleans Police Department's Metropolitan Orleans Total Information On-Line Network (MOTION). MOTION is being used for more than thirty law enforcement functions. MOTION provides criminal history on some 150,000 known offenders in the New Orleans Metropolitan area. It can match a suspect with criminal records via aliases, associates, MO, and addresses.

The other application is the New York City Police Department's Computer Assisted Terminal Criminal Hunt (CATCH). This computer system replaced the manual review of mug-shots by victims and witnesses. CATCH is capable of going through its database records and through a nickname, or MO, can provide a small number of suspects who fit the description. Consequently, the victim or witness only has to look at the viewing screen, projected from the microfilm, to find a match.

7

Accessed Information, Privacy, Dignity, and Security Laws

Law enforcement officers should be familiar with the rapidly increasing computer crime, counter measures, and laws that govern data, privacy, and dignity.

LAWS GOVERNING ACCESSED INFORMATION

In addition to the Wire Fraud Act, the Federal Computer Fraud and Abuse Act of 1986, and the Computer Security Act of 1987, most states have laws that cover unauthorized, illegal access and use of national security data, and private and sensitive information. This includes information on optical and magnetic disks, on tapes, on printouts, and in the computer. Because electronic data processing systems and networks are relatively new, there are not many federal and state laws concerning their use.

Wire Fraud Statute

The Wire Fraud Statute is defined under Title 18 U.S. Criminal Code, section 1343. It states that anyone who

"... devise(s) any scheme or artifice to defraud, or for obtaining money or property by means of false or fraudulent pretenses, representations, or promises, transmits or causes to be transmitted by means of wire, radio or television communication, in interstate or foreign commerce, any writings, signs, signals, pictures, or sounds for the purpose of executing such scheme or artifice . . ."

can get up to five years in prison and $1,000 fine for each transmission that crosses state lines in violation of this federal law. (The number of transmissions is considered quite important under this act.) Simply put, the Wire Fraud Statute prohibits the use of any modern communication media in connection with a fraudulent scheme if it involves interstate or foreign commerce, or both, or a national bank or financial institution that is insured by the federal government.

Computer Fraud and Abuse Act (1986)

The Computer Fraud and Abuse Act makes it a misdemeanor or felony (depending on the case) for any person to

". . . knowingly and willfully, directly or indirectly access or cause to be accessed any computer, computer system, computer network, . . . for the purpose of devising or executing any scheme or artifice to defraud, or obtain for themselves or another money, property, or services by means of false or fraudulent pretenses, representations, or promises . . . Or, knowingly and willfully, directly or indirectly access, alter, damage, or destroy any computer, computer system, or computer network . . ."

This act carries a fine up to $5,000 and a year in jail for a misdemeanor. The penalty for felony can be up to $10,000 and up to ten years in prison. Moreover, displaying unauthorized passwords on any electronic bulletin boards carries a maximum penalty of one year in jail for the first offense; ten years in prison for the second offense.

Computer Security Act (1987)

The Computer Security Act requires federal government agencies to develop detailed security plans, security training programs, and the identification of sensitive Federal Information Systems.

Most states, with the exception of Virginia and Vermont (as of this writing), have enacted legislation that cover unauthorized, illegal access and use of data on disks and tapes and in computers. For example, California has enacted the following laws, with more legislation in the wings.

California Penal Code 499c. This code covers trade secrets, theft, solicitation or bribery to acquire and/or communicate sensitive or proprietary information through unauthorized, illegal use of a computer system or telecommunications network.

Laws Governing Privacy, Dignity, and Security

California Penal Code 502. This code governs any sort of damage, copying (including documentation), use, alteration, disruption, or access of a computer, computer system, or computer network, for the purpose of fraud or embezzlement. This legislature, known as the Comprehensive Computer Data Access and Fraud Act, carries penalties of a fine up to $10,000 and/or imprisonment of up to three years.

The Public Record Act

The Public Record Act allows copies of records of an individual's employment history entered and stored at the Social Security Administration (SSA) database in Baltimore, Md., to be obtained with the particular person's written permission. Because everybody has to sign a permission to verify all facts and references whenever a person applies for a job, for a personal, automobile, real estate, or any other kind of a loan, or even when entering a hospital or other medical facility, almost anybody can get another individual's complete employment history from SSA.

Similarly, under this act, information contained on a person's driver license and any other information (tickets for traffic violations, driving under the influence, date of arrest and conviction (if applicable), etc.) that is entered and stored in the DMV database is available to a large segment of the population. Specifically, in addition to law enforcement, such information is regularly accessed by insurance agencies, credit service companies, and private investigators. However, private individuals can only obtain copies of their own records.

LAWS GOVERNING PRIVACY, DIGNITY, AND SECURITY

Laws assuring the privacy, dignity, and security of United States citizens, and allowing individuals to control and influence what information about them can be collected and stored, by whom, for what specific purpose, and to whom that information can be disclosed are perhaps more important than ever because of the all pervasive sophisticated computer systems. The following laws cover these issues:

The Fourth Amendment to the U.S. Constitution

The fourth amendment is, of course, one of the first and still the primary law to protect its citizens' privacy, dignity, and security. It states:

> "The right of the people to be secure in their persons, houses, papers, and effects, against unreasonable search and seizures, shall not be violated, and no Warrants shall issue, but upon *probable cause*, supported by Oath or affirmation, and *particularly*

describing the place to be searched, and the persons or things to be seized."

Simply put, no person, house, or property can be searched and seized without a warrant. A search warrant (based on an affidavit, i.e., a written and sworn to probable cause by a law enforcement officer, defining that "... a crime was committed, and that the suspect whose property is to be searched, committed the crime ...") is issued after it is signed by a judge or magistrate.

The fourth amendment, however, does not address possible exigent circumstances where the officers have probable cause to search a car or some other property and would lose the suspect if they would have to get a search warrant. For example, in *Carroll* v. *United States, 267 U.S. 132(1925)*, federal prohibition agents stopped a car traveling on a highway. The agents had probable cause to believe that bootleg liquor was hidden in the car. If they would have taken the time to get a search warrant, the car would have been long gone. So the officers searched the car on the spot. Subsequently, the Supreme Court held that the search of the car in that particular instance was reasonable because a car is movable. That is, by the time the agents would have obtained a warrant, the car (and its occupants) would have been able to leave the jurisdiction of the officers. To ensure, however, that the police could search and seize only in extraordinary conditions, in 1948 (*Johnson* v. *United States 333 U.S. 10*) the Supreme Court ruled that in the absence of exigent circumstances, searches are unconstitutional unless they are authorized by a search warrant.

There are other invoked exceptions to the search warrant requirement. One of the most common is a search that involves the *incident to arrest*. Under this precept, when a person is either under detention, or lawfully arrested, the police officer does not need to obtain a search or an arrest warrant to search the individual for weapons and/or evidence of crime.

Under detention means that the police have stopped the individual for questioning for a specific reason. Although no arrest is made, the person is not free to leave until the police informs him that he can.

The scope of this body search is for the protection of the officer. He can only pat down the individual to find out if there is any weapon, such as a gun, knife, club, or any other instrument that could possibly be used to assault the officer. The police officer can search the person's pockets only if the officer feels something that is likely to be a weapon.

Lawfully arrested means the police officer has probably cause to arrest the individual and to conduct a full search of the person, clothing, and containers found on him. If the person is arrested for felony, a strip search or visual search can be done at the time of booking or of entering the jail. A strip search is to be done in private by a person of the same sex

Laws Governing Privacy, Dignity, and Security

as the suspect. An officer cannot touch the suspect during this search. To legally search any body cavities, a search warrant specifying that intent must be obtained. If the individual was arrested for a misdemeanor that did not involve drugs, weapons, or violence, a strip search cannot be done.

Affirming this, in *United States* v. *Robinson, 414 U.S. 218 (1973)*, the Supreme Court held that the police can search any individual they have probable cause to arrest, regardless if it is for a minor infraction, such as traffic offense, or a serious crime. Similarly, if an officer stops a driver for minor violation (broken tail light, lapsed license plate, etc.), and during the process the officer notices some contraband in plain view, that provides the officer with probable cause to search the car in conjunction with incident to arrest.

The court based its ruling on the *bright line rules*. This doctrine frees the police officer from having to regard each situation as unique and requiring lengthy analysis. Instead, it allows the police officer to make on-the-spot judgment in familiar situations that can be considered as relatively minor invasions of privacy.

The bright line rules, however, have limitations. For example, in connection with incident to arrest, the police officer cannot search the entire home of the arrestee. As decided by the court in the *Chimely* v. *California, 395 U.S. 752 (1969)* case, the search has to be confined to the area within the arrested person's *immediate control*. Immediate control means the person's immediate surroundings within which he might be able to get to a weapon or destroy evidence. Another instance of such limitation can be seen in the *New York* v. *Belton, 453 U.S. 454 (1981)* case. The Supreme Court held that while under the bright line rules doctrine the police in an incident to arrest can search the inside of the arrestee's car, including the glove compartment, but can not search the locked trunk of the car. This is because the locked trunk is not ordinarily within the car occupant's immediate control. In such cases, the police officer can impound the car and search the trunk after a search warrant has been obtained.

Another circumstance in which search and seizure can be legal without a search warrant falls under the doctrine of *consent*. If a person voluntarily consents, that is, if he waives his constitutional right to the protection that the fourth amendment provides, and consents to have the police search his "person, house, papers, and effects," it legalizes an otherwise illegal search and seizure.

The Exclusionary Rule

Since our country was founded, the American courts have followed the *common law* doctrine of the English courts which, by the way, still prevails in the United Kingdom. This means that the result of a search and seizure (whether legally or illegally obtained) is admissible as evidence in a criminal court. In 1914, however, the Supreme Court in the landmark case of *Weeks* v. *United States* rejected the common law principle, and declared that illegally obtained evidence—i.e., evidence gathered in violation of the fourth amendment—justified that such evidence may not be used in federal courts.

The Supreme Court created the *exclusionary rule*. Then in 1961, in another landmark case, *Mapp* v. *Ohio*, the Supreme Court extended the exclusionary rule to every state and every court in the land. It based its decision on the meaning of the fourth, fifth, and fourteenth amendments which guarantees due process of law to any individual charged with a crime in state courts.

Note: It is important to remember that the exclusionary rule—a highly controversial and often debated issue—is not an amendment to the constitution. It is, however, an essential and abiding means by which the fourth, fifth, and fourteenth amendments are enforced. The exclusionary rule—as repeatedly affirmed by the Supreme Court—is not a personal constitutional right of the defendant. It is a judicial rule that attempts to deter law enforcement officials from violating the fourth amendment by barring illegally obtained evidence.

The effectiveness of the rule, however, is open to debate. Even its creator, the Supreme Court, had to admit that it has "acted in the absence of convincing empirical evidence and relied, instead, on its own assumptions of human nature and the interrelationship of the various components of the law enforcement system" (Criminal Justice Ethics 1, Summer/Fall 1982).

Before discussing the pros and cons of the Exclusionary Rule, perhaps a review of the affected amendments would be helpful. Because the fourth amendment was quoted earlier, here are the salient parts of the fifth and the fourteenth amendments.

The Fifth Amendment states, "... nor shall (any person) be compelled in any criminal case to be a witness against himself, nor be deprived of life, liberty, or property without due process of law ..."

The Fourteenth Amendment states, "... No State shall make or enforce any law which shall abridge the privileges or immunities of citizens of the United States; nor shall any State deprive any person of life, liberty, or property, without due process of law; nor deny to any person within its jurisdiction the equal protection of the laws ..."

The pros of the Exclusionary Rule are:

- It requires that evidence obtained in violation of the accused's constitutional rights not to be acceptable in federal or state courts.
- It discourages law enforcement officers from unlawful invasion of privacy and dignity of the defendant in a criminal proceeding.

Laws Governing Privacy, Dignity, and Security

- It prevents a witness to testify as to the intent or the state of mind of the defendant.

The cons of the Exclusionary Rule are:

- It has little or no value in deterring law enforcement misconduct. Some years back, Chief Justice Warren Burger said, "I suggest that the notion that suppression of evidence in a given case effectively deters the future action of the particular policeman, or policemen generally, was never more than wishful thinking on the part of the Courts."
- It frees the guilty, and thus destroys the public's respect for the law and the courts. Justice Benjamin Cardozo expressed many people's chagrin when he said, ". . . the criminal is to go free because the constable has blundered."
- Police officers cannot be expected to understand and comply with the exclusionary rule when even the Supreme Court judges cannot agree on its finer points.
- It is not a part of the constitution.

In the 1984 cases of *United States* v. *Leon* and *Massachusetts* v. *Sheppard*, the Supreme Court ruled that in these specific cases where the search warrants were invalid there was an exception to the exclusionary rule because the police officers were not aware of the invalidity of the warrants. Thus, the *good faith* exception to the exclusionary rule was created. In the good faith search—whether it is in relation to an incident to arrest, or in plain view, or other good faith circumstances—it is up to the defendant to prove that the officer did not act in good faith when conducting an otherwise unconstitutional search and seizure.

The Privacy Act of 1974

This act allows individuals to control and influence what information about them can be collected and stored, by which government agency, for what specific reason, and to whom that information can be disclosed. Also, this act allows individuals to challenge the accuracy of any information about them, and file a statement indicating the errors and asking for a correction. The specific agency must respond within ten days. If the agency does not respond, a judicial review follows. If a correction is agreed to by the agency, or ordered by a judge, the agency must notify the organizations to whom the original inaccurate information about the individual was disclosed.

The drawback of this act is that if a particular agency doesn't honor the private citizen's request, it is the individual who has to enforce the act by taking the case to court.

Accessed Information, Privacy, Dignity, and Security Laws

The Fair Credit Reporting Act of 1975

This act is an addendum to the Privacy Act. It states that if an investigative consumer report is done on a prospective employee, customer, or client, that individual must have access to the information collected. If the report is incorrect, it is the individual's right to ask a correction of the error(s) under the Privacy Act. If the particular company/organization is unwilling to do so, the Bureau of Consumer Protection (Federal Trade Commission, Washington, D.C. 20850) will help settle the matter.

The Freedom of Information Act

The Freedom of Information Act, enacted in 1967 and amended in 1974, provides private individuals the right to have access to declassified government and legal information. To be more precise, if an individual requests information from any agency of the executive branch of the federal government, the agency must provide the requested information, as long as it is declassified. Furthermore, under this act, trial transcripts and disposition of criminal cases are available to private individuals, just as to the police.

The drawback of this act in obtaining government information is identical to the Privacy Act. In both cases the individual is the one who has to take the uncooperative agency to court to enforce the law.

8

Computer Crime's Impact on Automated Systems

Digital computer systems have become ubiquitous in all types of facilities, from government and commercial corporations to academia, to criminal justice and law enforcement agencies. Since in the past ten years almost every type of organization has been victimized by computer crime, it is essential for law enforcement practitioners to understand what constitutes computer crime and who are the potential perpetrators.

Of course, with law enforcement professionals becoming more computer literate, and with government and commercial organizations realizing the devastating effect of computer crime, law enforcement professionals have a better chance of catching—if not deterring—a computer criminal. Yet, as the recent virus epidemic that struck some 6,200 computer systems across the country and is still being battled in California's Silicon Valley proves, it is imperative for law enforcement officials to keep up with the latest technology against computer crime. Even then, there is always a good chance that someone will come up with a way to beat the system.

As to the actual modus operandi of this purely twentieth century crime, following are eight basic categories of computer crime.

SOFTWARE PIRACY

Software piracy is the least publicized, yet most common, computer crime. It impacts industry, government, criminal justice, and academia to the tune of millions of dollars annually.

Software piracy is the copying or theft of proprietary computer software and/or raw data or information. Moreover, if the criminal just copies the valuable software or sensitive data, it's almost impossible to detect the crime because the original software or data remains on the disk or tape, or in the computer.

In a recent interesting case in Palo Alto, California, a senior systems analyst copied the company's proprietary software before resigning from his position. Shortly afterward he set up his own software firm. He manufactured and sold the somewhat modified and improved stolen software for half of the original price. When a year later the rightful owner of the original software became aware of the theft, he started litigation against his ex-employee. However, under questioning by the defendant's attorney, he had to admit that his original software was still on his disks. And consequently the original owner lost the case because he could not legally prove that his ex-employee stole his proprietary software.

In many other software piracy cases data processing employees copy or steal programs and/or valuable information to sell to the company's competitor, to a foreign government, or a businessman who wants to save a lot of time, money, and effort in research and development. Most of such in-house criminals perpetrate such crimes because they need money for gambling or drugs, or they are simply greedy. However, they also are quite aware that it's difficult to prove such crime, and so they can get away with it.

Individuals, however, don't have a patent on software piracy as a recent lawsuit proves. In that specific case, police officers, backed by a search warrant, seized boxes of illegally copied software in a raid on a San Francisco Bay area computer company. The software organizations that accused the company of violating copyrights included the biggest names in the software field: Ashton-Tate, Microsoft Corp., Lotus Development Corp., and WordPerfect Corp.

Potential Perpetrators

Because only data processing professionals have the skill and the authorization to access proprietary software and/or secret or sensitive data, potential perpetrators have to be experienced programmers, systems analysts, programmer/analysts, systems programmers, or EDP auditors. This holds true whether the person illegally copies a proprietary software for himself, for another person, or for a company.

COMPUTER-AIDED FRAUD AND EMBEZZLEMENT

Computer-aided fraud and embezzlement is the automated version of the good old-fashioned manual fraud or embezzlement that has been going on for centuries by unscrupulous employees.

Computer-Aided Fraud and Embezzlement

According to the June 9, 1987, statement of the Federal Reserve Board and other bank regulators in Washington, D.C., "Serious computer-assisted fraud and embezzlement by insiders have contributed significantly to about one-third of U.S. bank failures in recent years."

As if to underscore this comment, in February 1989, the Secret Service, acting on an informer's tip, raided an apartment in Long Beach, California, and thus foiled a bank programmer's scheme to steal $14 million from hundreds of Bank of America automated teller (ATM) machines. The 28-year-old programmer's area of responsibility was to maintain ATM accounts. When he decided to get rich quick, he recorded thousands of names, IDs, and passwords. Then, with a few friends, he made up thousands of fictitious ATM cards. The plan was to milk Bank of America ATM machines all over the state during the coming three-day holiday. The scheme would have worked too, except that one of the perpetrator's cohorts got cold feet and called the authorities.

Another textbook case of such insider's computer-aided embezzlement is the $21.4 million that Ross Eugene Fields, Sammy Marshall and Lloyd Benjamin Lewis "liberated" from a Los Angeles branch of Wells Fargo Bank in 1981.

Lewis was the assistant operations officer at the Beverly Hills branch of the bank and a friend of Fields, an ex-convict and an outstanding promoter of scams. Fields convinced Lewis and another friend, Marshall, who worked at another branch of the bank, that he had a fail-safe "rollover" plan to get money from the bank.

The ingenious scam that bypassed the bank's internal computer accounting system and tapped into the bank's rich interbranch settlement fund went something like this:

Whenever Fields wrote out a check, or whenever a cashier's check in amounts anywhere from $19,000 to $250,000 was issued for him by Lewis, the assistant operations officer offset the debit with false credit. (Fields had a checking account at the bank with less than $50.) Lewis, by misencoding the standard two-part interbranch settlement form before entering the transaction into the computer, was able to counter all the debit with nonexistent credit from another bank branch where Marshall worked before he quit. Thus, the bank's computer system, which was designed to check the credit transactions from each issuing branch and the corresponding debit transactions from each receiving branch before processing the daily transactions, was fooled. That is, with the debits and credits seemingly balanced, the bank's interbranch computer system accepted Lewis's transactions for processing.

The bottom line was that between September, 1978 and January, 1981, Lewis funneled some $21.3 million out of the bank, with most of the money going into the hands of his good friend, Fields.

Computer Crime's Impact on Automated Systems

Lewis was able to continue with this grand-scale embezzlement for almost three years by never being late or absent from work, and by not taking a vacation all through this period.

Then on January 14, 1981, something happened. And the scheme that worked so well for almost three years came to an abrupt end. Lewis was never able to explain just exactly what he did wrong. But the fact of the matter was that the bank's computer system detected an anomaly in the interbranch settlement funds, and red flagged Lewis's transaction on that day.

Subsequently, the transactions were examined carefully by the bank's auditors, and on January 23, 1981, Lewis' supervisor and the branch manager confronted the assistant operations officer with unassailable proof of his illegal activities.

Lewis fled in panic. But after thinking it over, and contrary to the advice of Fields and Marshall, he went to the nearest FBI office and turned himself in. Even though he turned state's evidence against Fields and Marshall, Lewis was convicted, and on June 1, 1982, he was sentenced to five years in federal prison. And while Fields was sentenced to eight years, Marshall received only five years in federal prison. (None of them served more than two years.)

Potential Perpetrators

This type of computer crime is usually perpetrated by skilled data processing professionals. However, if a user knows the system, a non-computer employee can pull off a computer-aided fraud or embezzlement as well. That is, as long as he has access to certain applications or records.

DATA MANIPULATION

Data manipulation is simply adding or changing data prior to or during the process of entering data into the computer system. This type of computer crime is a favorite of office workers who are computer literate, use the system for their daily work, and need money to pay their debts or drug habits. The modus operandi of data manipulation is adding fictitious claims or accounts into the accounts payable; setting up a fictitious account; and sending the claims checks or checks for the account payable amounts to the fictitious account.

With Janet Blair, one of the multitude of Social Security Administration employees in Baltimore, who used a desktop computer to issue instructions to the agency's computer system to generate SSA checks, it was a different story. Her motivation to commit computer-assisted fraud was not to gain money for herself. It seems a couple of her friends were in a financial bind, and so Blair decided to add her friends' names to the next series of computer instructions for the computer system to generate SSA checks. To be more precise, Blair entered instructions for the issuance of fraudulent checks for her friends via her mainframe-connected intelligent terminal. Then, to avoid detection, as soon as the computer printed the checks, she entered a command to erase the audit trail of her illegal transactions.

Blair gave away $102,000 in SSA checks before she was caught. The fraud was detected not by SSA auditors, but by an alert Philadelphia bank official who became suspicious of a large number of cashed SSA checks made out to different names but having the same Social Security number: Blair's. She was convicted and sentenced to eight years in a federal prison, in addition to a fine of $500.

Potential Perpetrators

This type of computer crime can be perpetrated by anybody (if there are no skilled EDP auditors monitoring transactions and no rigorous system controls) from programmer/analysts, computer operators, data entry operators, and end users.

SALAMI TECHNIQUE

This type of computer crime is alive and well in banks, savings & loans, insurance companies, financial institutions, and organizations that handle pension funds or union accounts. In fact, many EDP auditors admit that the salami technique is the simplest and safest way to steal via a computer system, especially if the perpetrator works for a large company.

The salami technique consists of reducing—either by a slight change in certain programs, or by inserting extra instructions into programs—interest-bearing accounts by a couple of pennies or even fractions when calculating interests/dividends, and then transferring the amounts to an account under an assumed name. Because the customers/members' accounts are rounded down to the nearest cent, the accounts are balanced, and the EDP auditor—unless alerted by an informer—is satisfied and is not looking for any discrepancy.

Potential Perpetrators

Programmer/analysts, systems analysts, systems programmers, and EDP auditors are the only ones who have sufficient skills and access to financial applications to pull off such computer crime.

SCAVENGING

Scavenging is a method of obtaining data or information by searching trash cans of companies' data processing departments, offices, or retail

Computer Crime's Impact on Automated Systems

stores. This is called physical scavenging. There also is the electronic scavenging that involves searching for residual data left in a computer.

Physical scavenging of trash containing computer printouts, forms, and code-sheets, put out on the street by DP facilities for garbage collection is the most favored method for hackers to get IDs, passwords, and other vital information.

Electronic scavenging is more insidious. This is done when a programmer with high level of authorization leaves his terminal unattended allowing another programmer with a low level of authorization access to the terminal and the system.

Potential Perpetrators

Janitors, ground keepers, outsiders, or just about anybody can be a potential perpetrator of physical scavenging. As for electronic scavenging, any DP professional or even an end user can be potential perpetrators, as long as some programmer working on a sensitive application or file leaves his terminal unattended.

TROJAN HORSE

This type of computer-aided crime, which consists of covertly inserting unauthorized instructions into a production program, might be done to achieve material gains; to sabotage a program and botch up the system; or to have some "fun." The last category is usually done to see if a few extra instructions can have any impact on the performance of a program. Whatever the reason, this computer crime effects a monetary loss to the organization.

Barry Wyche, a computer operator at the University of Maryland Hospital, Baltimore, was arrested some four months after he was hired. He was charged with embezzling $40,000 by inserting false invoices into the hospital's accounts payable production programs. Wyche was caught by an alert supervisor. Subsequently, he was indicted, convicted, and sentenced to five years in the Maryland Division of Correction.

After Wyche was arrested, the hospital officials were chagrined to learn that the man not only had a criminal record, but that he was on probation for an identical offense at the time the hospital hired him.

Potential Perpetrators

Systems programmers, programmers/analysts, computer operators, and end users are possible perpetrators.

TIME (OR LOGIC) BOMB OR TRAP DOOR

Although the technique is somewhat similar to the trojan horse, the goal of a time, or logic, bomb or trap door is always sabotage. Specifically, the covert instructions are written and inserted into a production program. These instructions are triggered to be executed at a specific time by a predefined date or condition. A logic bomb can erase specified program(s) or file(s), or cause an application software, such as payroll or accounts receivable, or the whole system, to crash. Because the execution of the instructions can be programmed so that it is delayed anywhere from one month to a year, by the time the sabotage actually occurs, the perpetrator is usually long gone from the company, if not the area.

A time bomb is almost impossible to detect or prevent, and it is almost impossible to catch the person who devised it because a clever programmer can write the instructions so that when the bomb erases the target program, application, or system, it destroys itself as well.

This is exactly what happened last year at a midwestern city's Water and Power Department. An employee in the data processing department was fired for unsatisfactory work performance, and told to leave in two weeks. Before the disgruntled programmer left, he wrote and inserted a time bomb into one of the organization's databases. The program was written so that it would erase a number of valuable applications three months after he received his severance paycheck.

As a final touch of his vendetta, when he said goodbye to one of his colleagues he mentioned that he left behind a time bomb. He didn't, however, say which database or what applications he targeted.

The utility company called the authorities, who in turn called some computer crime experts. Nevertheless, the time bomb was not found. And when three months later the bomb did its work, law enforcement officials could not prosecute the man because the bomb destroyed itself after erasing some valuable applications.

VIRUS OR WORM

A virus is the latest and the most destructive type of identified computer crime. A computer virus or worm program has the capability of instantaneously cloning a copy of itself and burying that copy inside other programs just before it erases programs or an application, and just before it destroys itself. A virus also can spread from computer to computer system over the telephone lines and electronic bulletin boards. It can damage the computer's memory and knock out the total system.

A computer virus or worm is deadly because it can slide through bar-

Computer Crime's Impact on Automated Systems

riers that are currently used to control access to sensitive and valuable information, and thought up till now to be crime proof.

The latest virus case involves Robert Morris, Jr., a 23-year-old Cornell University computer science student who, in November 1988, was able to affect 6,200 computer systems—including national defense and research systems—across the country by inserting a virus program into the Internet computer network. The self-professed hacker's virus program cost the nation millions of dollars in down-time and rebuilding the systems. Subsequently, he was charged, convicted, and sentenced for the crime.

Potential Perpetrators

Outside hackers, as well as inside people such as DP professionals are potential perpetrators.

Note: Although most people use virus and worm interchangeably, to be precise a *virus* is a piece of code that is added to other programs, including the operating system. It, however, cannot run independently. It requires its host program to be run to activate it. Thus, it is analogous to biological viruses that are not truly live, yet they invade the host cells and take them over, making them produce new viruses. A *worm* on the other hand, is a program that can run by itself and can propagate a full working version of itself in other systems.

A POSTSCRIPT

In February 1989, the first hacker was brought to trial and convicted under the Computer Fraud and Abuse Act of 1986 in Chicago, H.D. Zinn, Jr., an 18-year-old hacker was sentenced to nine months in federal prison with no opportunity for parole, and fined $10,000 for illegally penetrating the computer systems of AT&T and the U.S. Department of Defense.

Specifically, Zinn was convicted for copying $1.2 million worth of programs, and destroying the files valued at $174,000. In addition, he posted passwords, phone numbers, and directions on how to breach AT&T's computer system on the hackers' underground electronic bulletin board.

9

Physical Security

To counteract computer crime in all its forms, organizations, including law enforcement agencies, must set up and maintain an effective computer security program. Although each organization's security requirements are unique, physical security is the first line of prevention against unlawful entry into any facility. Thus, physical security should be one of the many components in a carefully planned overall security system to protect the hardware and software, as well as the sensitive data contained on magnetic and optical disks, magnetic tapes, and in the computers of the criminal justice and law enforcement agencies. A well-established and well-maintained physical security provides the accountability to effect a climate of security.

RISK ANALYSIS

A risk analysis must be undertaken before any security system can be developed and before any security standards can be established. (See FIG. 9-1.) Risk analysis is a systematic study that examines the facility's assets and areas vulnerable to criminal activities and recommends countermeasures based on cost/benefit analysis. It can be conducted in the following structured way:

- Identify and evaluate all hardware, software, and operations in terms of replacement cost, processing/interruption cost, and the cost of obtaining temporary outside hardware and software (See FIG. 9-2).
- Define the volume and dollar statistics of all computer systems in the facility.
- Define the official positions that need high level authorization to access sensitive data.
- Analyze fraud potentials in vulnerable systems and applications.

Physical Security

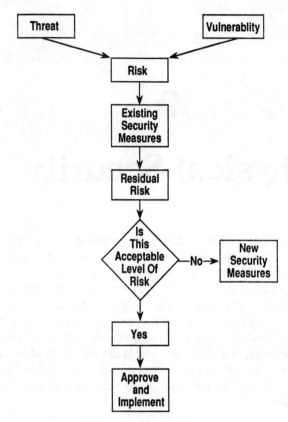

Fig. 9-1. Risk analysis process.

To show a simple example of how a properly conducted risk analysis looks, an abbreviated risk assessment of the ATM (Automated Teller Machine) is presented in FIGS. 9-3 through 9-6.

Physical security to be efficient should consist of the following measures:

BUILDING AND PARKING LOT SECURITY

Building and parking lot security might include:

- A well-lighted entrance and parking lot
- No signs to advertise the fact that the building houses a criminal justice or law enforcement data processing facility
- No windows on the first two floors of the DP center
- Security guards patrolling the parking lot at irregular intervals, especially at night

Analyst: (Name)			Date:
Procedures Performed	Yes	No	Comments (if "no" is checked)
Evaluation of all hardware			
Definition of the volume and $$ statistics of vital systems & applications			
Evaluation of the above + all other business-sensitive systems			
Definition of high level authorization staff positions			
Analysis of fraud potentials in vulnerable systems & applications			
Determination of possible penetration of computer security			
Compilation of possible expected annual loss			
Cost/Benefit Analysis			

Fig. 9-2. Risk analysis checklist.

Physical Security

Category of adverse consequences	Elements to consider	Risk Level		
		Low	Medium	High
Disruption of internal operations and control	—Effects on department or group —Effects on company —Information for decision making			
Reduced employee morale	—Physical environment —Productivity —Grievances —Esprit —Turnover			
Direct adverse effect on financial results	—Company revenue level and growth —Investment required —Expenses			
Inadequate user/cust. service	—Image of MIS department —Existing/potential users/customers			
Disruption of vendor relations or timely supply of goods and services	—Stability/reliability of source of supply —Purchasing cost-effectiveness —Importance of vendor			

Fig. 9-3. Guidelines for risk assessment.

PHYSICAL ACCESS CONTROL

Effective access control is a key step in maintaining DP center security. To prevent forced entry, violence, or unauthorized persons entering the facility, the following security measures are essential:

- Security guards in the lobby
- Receptionist behind a bullet-proof glass
- Magnetic ID cards or badges given to permanent and temporary employees working in the building to be scrutinized by the guards before allowing entrance into the building

Security guards in the lobby or any secure facility should be instructed to be especially careful in examining the ID cards of temporary

- Hardware
  1. Total replacement costs $150,000.00
  2. Weekly use of backup hardware   2,000.00
- Software
  1. Total replacement costs   300,000.00
- Business
  1. Total weekly business
     Interruption costs   400,000.00
- Staff Positions with High-Level
  Authorization
  1. Accounting personnel   200,000.00
  2. Payroll personnel   300,000.00
  3. Purchasing personnel   100,000.00
  4. Admitting personnel   50,000.00
                        TOTAL: $1,502,000.00

- Fraud potentials in vulnerable systems and applications
  1. Illegal transaction through use of lost or stolen magnetic card and password
  2. Misappropriation of magnetic card and password by staff
  3. Data manipulation by staff
  4. Trojan Horse—insertion of unauthorized instructions into a production program by staff
  5. Time Bomb—sabotage by staff
  6. Rounding down by staff
  7. Scavenging by staff or nonemployees
  8. Piggybacking by staff or nonemployees
  9. Computer security breach by staff
  10. Natural disasters

Fig. 9-4. Risk assessment.

Risk No.	Est. Yrly. Occurrence	Est. $ Loss/ Occurrence	Annual Expected Loss
1	4	$1,000.00	$4,000.00
2	3	$10,000.00	$30,000.00
3	2	$25,000.00	$50,000.00
4	1	$10,000.00	$10,000.00
5	.10	$50,000.00	$5,000.00
6	.25	$10,000.00	$2,500.00
7	1	$5,000.00	$5,000.00
8	1	$5,000.00	$5,000.00
9	1	$25,000.00	$25,000.00
10	.25	$100,000.00	$25,000.00

TOTAL ANNUAL EXPECTED LOSS IN DOLLARS: $161,500.00

Fig. 9-5. Executed annual loss.

employees and consultants to see if the cards are still valid. Better yet, the organization should have an iron-clad policy that no final paycheck can be given to any employee or consultant before the individual's ID card or badge is turned in.

Physical Security

Item	Capital Investment/ Startup Costs	Annual Operating Costs	Annual Loss Avoidance
Magnetic strip cards	$ 2,000.00	$ 500.00	$ 10,000.00
Internal EDP auditor	——	50,000.00	80,000.00
External EDP auditor	——	10,000.00	40,000.00
Training program for personnel	2,000.00	1,000.00	40,000.00
Paper shredders	500.00	50.00	10,000.00
Personnel background investigation	2,000.00	500.00	40,000.00
IBM's R.A.C.F.	50,000.00	1,000.00	80,000.00
TOTAL:	$56,500.00	$63,050.00	$300,000.00

$$\text{Expected Annual Return on Expenditures for Countermeasures} = \frac{300,000 - 63,050}{63,050} \times 100 = 376\%$$

As a result, based upon the expected annual return, all of the above-mentioned countermeasures are recommended because of the considerably low cost of implementation. In fact, the previously mentioned computer security breach profit was $90,000; a profit that would have been sufficient to institute these control measures and prevent similar crimes.

Fig. 9-6. Cost/benefit analysis.

A classical example of a DP facility's physical access control being penetrated with an invalid ID card is the infamous case of Stanley Mark Rifkin.

On October 25, 1978, Rifkin, a computer consultant, defrauded Security Pacific Bank in Los Angeles of $10.2 million. Rifkin was able to do that because, though he finished his consulting assignment for the bank in May, 1978, the security guard in the lobby of the DP center did not examine the consultant's invalid ID card as he strolled through the lobby and into the facility.

Once past the security guard, Rifkin walked directly to the wire transfer room, the inner sanctum of the organization, the heart of the electronic funds transfer (EFT) operations. Rifkin was familiar with the wire transfer room, its staff, and its operations, because his previous assignment was to design an alternate EFT computer system as a backup. In fact, it came to light later, it was during his assignment that Rifkin got the idea of robbing the bank via the very electronic system he was paid to protect by a backup.

At the door of the wire transfer room Rifkin identified himself, and told the supervisor that he was on another assignment to study "how the system could be improved." The supervisor remembered him, and thus Rifkin entered the highly sensitive area. Subsequently, he walked around the room with a notebook in his hand, seemingly noting the sequence of operation, and jotting down several data including the secret transfer code of the day that (just as he remembered) was displayed in plain view on the wall. Even back in those days the secret code by which millions of dollars were transferred from one branch to another, from one bank to another in the United States and globally by authorized upper management was changed daily by the administrator. The only problem was that nobody followed up on this critical security measure to see how the daily secret transfer code was handled in the wire transfer room; the hub of EFT operations. Specifically, nobody bothered to inform the wire transfer room supervisor of the high risk factor of the code and the importance of not displaying publicly the secret code.

Having obtained that particular day's secret transfer code for EFT, Rifkin waved goodbye to the staff and walked out of the bank. On the street he went to the nearest pay telephone booth and called the wire transfer room that he just left.

When one of the EFT operators answered, Rifkin—giving the name of an executive from the international department of the bank whom he met during his assignment, and after providing that day's secret transfer code—instructed the operator to transfer $10.2 million to Wozchod Handelsbank, a Swiss bank in Zurich, Switzerland. The stated amount was to be credited to the account of Russalmaz Agency, Geneva, Switzerland. The operator, having observed all the correct procedures, told Rifkin that his order will be taken care of immediately, and, as required, gave him the transaction number.

The next morning Rifkin flew to Geneva, Switzerland. In Geneva, through a Los Angeles diamond broker's contact, he met the Soviet wholesale diamond agency's director. Rifkin wanted to buy diamonds for the full $10.2 million he stole because he believed that they were highly salable commodities back in the States. The Soviet diamond agency, however, had only $8,145,000 worth of diamonds on hand. The Russian director did not want to sell to Rifkin until the Russalmaz Agency's bank notified him that the proper amount was credited to its account.

Rifkin was ready to pick up the diamonds, but the ever cautious Russian director did not directly hand over the merchandise. He gave Rifkin a claim ticket for a piece of baggage to be picked up at the duty-free Geneva airport. The next day, before boarding his plane back to the states, Rifkin retrieved a plain, much-used canvas bag with the claim ticket.

In Luxembourg, where he arranged to have a stopover, Rifkin—with his expensive leather luggage and the contrasting shabby canvas bag—took a taxi to the best hotel in town. In the hotel room Rifkin locked the door; gently placed the bulky bag on the bed; opened and emptied its contents slowly; and for the first time he saw the $8.2 million worth of polished diamonds he bought. He was fascinated by the sparkling stones poured over the bedcover.

Being a practical man, Rifkin now folded the empty canvas bag and

Physical Security

placed it on the bottom of his luggage. Next, he tightly repacked the diamonds and placed them under a couple of neatly folded underclothes and dress shirts, and closed his suitcase.

The following morning the euphoric Rifkin boarded his plane for New York City where, according to his carefully worked out plan, he was to embark on the next stage of his becoming an instant millionaire. At the John F. Kennedy airport, however, he had a few tense moments when he had to go through customs. But the customs officials had no reason to turn over every piece of the typically middle-class Rifkin's neatly packed suitcase, and so they missed the diamonds.

From New York City Rifkin flew to Rochester where he tried to prevail upon an old friend to open and run a wholesale diamond brokerage in New York City. Rifkin just wanted to be the silent partner who funded the business. The story that Rifkin told his friend was that he just came back from Europe (true) where he was involved in a large real estate operation (false), and that his share of the profit was paid partly in currency but mostly in polished diamonds. To convince his friend that he was serious about the deal, Rifkin gave the man $6,000 in cash. Rifkin's friend, an executive at a local company, promised to think over the attractive offer.

The same day, however, the electronic theft was discovered by the executive from the International Department of the Security Pacific Bank whose name Rifkin used to perpetrate his computer crime. Subsequently the FBI was called in to find Rifkin and the stolen millions.

News of the theft, together with a picture of the fugitive was featured on the evening TV news on November 3, 1978, and Rifkin's friend saw it. Not wanting to be involved in any criminal activity, he immediately called Security Pacific Bank officials in Los Angeles and the chief FBI agent in Rochester. The subsequent plan was to arrest the fugitive the next morning when Rifkin and his friend were to meet to further discuss Rifkin's offer.

But Rifkin also saw the broadcast, and he took a plane that same night out of Rochester and back to California. His flight was to no avail, however. On November 7, 1978, Rifkin was arrested in Carlsbad, California, at the home of another unsuspecting friend.

On March 26, 1979, the Honorable William Matthew Byrne, Jr., Judge in Los Angeles, sentenced Rifkin to eight years in federal prison. (Rifkin was released after two-and-a-half years.)

Postscript 1: Security Pacific Bank got back most of the currency stolen by Rifkin, and all of the diamonds. The bank, however, had to pay a large fine to U.S. Customs for being "the current owner of almost $8.2 million polished diamonds smuggled into the country."

Postscript 2: After his release, Rifkin became a much sought after computer consultant. In fact, in August 1984, he was hired by the American Institute for the Advancement of Science to automate the organization's operations. And in the ensuing years Rifkin was nominated an officer in the local chapter of one of the most prestigious professional scientific associations.

A recent example of a supposedly tightly controlled security area being penetrated is the case of the thefts of two microcomputers on two consecutive nights from the Star Wars anti-missile program offices in the Pentagon, in June 1988. According to Pentagon officials, it appears to be an inside job.

The first theft occurred between Friday evening and Saturday morning; the second theft occurred between the same evening and Sunday morning. According to Pentagon investigators there are two possible scenarios: The thief or thieves were able to enter the facility and perpetrate the crime without detection because the Video cameras had not been loaded that evening—a common occurrence in the high-security office. Or a SDIO employee with the proper clearance entered the complex through the main lobby where a guard was on duty, but then left with the computers through a basement security door that is under Video camera surveillance, but not guarded.

Postscript: The Star Wars office complex is one of the few areas of the Pentagon building that is off-limits to those without a special security pass in addition to the normal building pass. That any thefts occurred just proves the significance of having an efficient physical security.

- Visitors' ID badges and log books. Visitors should be given a visitor's badge and asked to sign the log book, specifying the employee they are visiting, as well as the date and time of their arrival. The DP staff should escort the visitor to the designated person.

    A cardinal rule for effective computer crime deterrence is that a visitor cannot go anywhere in a DP facility unless accompanied by an employee. When a visitor leaves the facility, the temporary badge must be returned to the receptionist, and the time of his departure recorded in the log book.
- Intrusion detection devices. Cameras and/or closed-circuit TV should monitor entrances to high risk areas.
- Facility access. Within the facility, sensitive areas, such as the computer room, data library, I/O room, and the like, should have a single entry door (not counting the emergency doors) and an electronic door lock to ensure that it is accessible to authorized personnel only.
- Access control systems. To begin with, a properly designed and installed access control system reduces risks, security costs, and

Physical Security

secures the working environment. Specifically, by being selective as to who can access sensitive areas, valuable data and information are protected, and potential crime reduced.

Most access control systems operate in a *proximity mode*. That is, authorized access to an area is gained when an electronically coded proximity access card is presented within two to four inches of a sensor installed in the door. Because of the proximity nature of the sensor/access card interface, the access card—which contains tuned circuits—does not have to be removed from the purse or wallet, minimizing the incidence of lost or stolen cards. Moreover, the proximity card is durable because the sensing elements are encased in vandal-proof, dirt-proof, weather-proof, and shock-resistant material. Such access control system costs more than the traditional system that relies on magnetic-strip card. The price of a proximity mode access control system that includes an access control sensor device near the door and an electronically coded card can run from $1,000 to $5,000. The advantages of such a system, however, are many. In addition to controlling access to a sensitive area, the proximity access control system also can be tied to a computer to provide an audit trail of the time that employees are entering and leaving the secured area. The system can be set up to activate a video camera that photographs all persons entering and leaving the sensitive area.

FIRE SECURITY/PROTECTION

Fire is a serious threat to DP facilities. According to insurance companies, fire is the most frequent cause of damage and loss. When there is more attention paid to fire protection, there is less risk involved, and consequently the criminal justice or law enforcement agency pays less insurance premiums.

Facilities with computer systems operations should employ these fire prevention measures:

- All walls, floors, and ceilings should have a minimum of two-hour fire rating; that is, they should be able to "take" fire for up to two hours.
- Safes that store tapes, disks, records, and documentation should have a minimum of four-hour fire rating.
- Access/emergency doors to the outside should have automatic panic-hardware and self-closing devices. There should be no entrance to the computer/machine room or the tape library from the outside.

- The fire alarm should be wired so that it rings simultaneously at the DP facility and the nearest fire department.
- Fire alarm signals should be located where prompt response is assured, such as in well-traveled corridors, or the coffee room.
- Fusible link (any easily fused metal) actuated fire dampers—such as lead metal—should be used to close all heating and air-conditioning ducts in the computer/machine room.
- Automatic smoke and ionization detection systems should be installed in the ceiling, and a water detection system (in case the air conditioning unit breaks down) should be installed under the raised floor of the computer/machine room.
- Halon 1301[1] or some similar system should be installed throughout the computer/machine room. (Halon is a Du Pont trade name from an extinguishing agent that controls fire but does not damage machines, nor does it replace oxygen. It mixes with oxygen.) Halon requires detection system actuation and automatic interlocking with air conditioning and computer power to maintain gas concentration and remove the source of electrical ignition.
- Smoke detection and Halon or some similar system should be provided for under the floor areas in the tape library and other sensitive areas.
- Air ducts of the air conditioning units should be secured against access (burglary or gas bomb) by heavy-gauge screens, and the air intake should be monitored by a special device for gaseous substances.
- Master controls for utilities such as electric power, lights, air conditioner, and water should be located in controlled access areas.
- Emergency lighting for safe evacuation in case of fire or other disaster should be provided in all areas of the facility.

CONTINGENCY AND DISASTER RECOVERY PLANS

No chapter on fire protection and security for criminal justice and law enforcement DP facilities is complete without discussing contingency and disaster recovery plans. To ensure that critical data and information on disks and tapes and in the computers of government and private organizations is protected and can be recovered promptly in case of a disaster, a

---

[1] Because after many years of research it has been determined that Halon gas is a potent depleter of the earth's protective ozone layer, the U.S. Environmental Agency endorsed the *Montreal Protocol* in July 1989. This international treaty requires the phase out of Halon by the year 2005 in all U.S. and other countries' computer facilities. Consequently, water sprinklers and carbon dioxide fire-fighting equipment might make a comeback.

Physical Security

contingency plan and a comprehensive disaster recovery plan must be in place.

A Contingency Plan

A contingency plan identifies the crucial information systems and applications that are vital for the organization to be able to function. The plan also determines how often (daily, weekly, or biweekly) those identified systems and applications have to run on the computer, specifically which software programs are essential for the organization, and at what intervals they are to be processed. The contingency plan also identifies vulnerable areas and sensitive positions. The contingency plan should be based on risk analysis.

Further, the contingency plan addresses the concern of the effect of a natural, technical, or man-made disaster, including bomb threat, on the organization's operations. The plan determines which systems and applications would have the highest priorities to be run on the backup, off-site hot site or cold site. (Definition later in this chapter.)

A contingency plan identifies the organization's information resource systems; ascertains the impact of interruption or loss of dataprocessing on the organization's operations should a disaster occur; and defines the off-site operations sequence of critical systems on a computer that has been tested at regular intervals to ensure that the software runs on it properly.

A realistic contingency plan will not only minimize the impact of an emergency, regardless of its degree of severity, but also act as a deterrence and detection against computer crime.

A Disaster Recovery Plan

A disaster recovery plan is a precise set of written procedures that instructs all employees in that particular facility exactly what to do—within their own sphere of responsibility—if a natural, technical, or man-made disaster (or the threat of a disaster) occurs.

A rigorous, published, tested, and continuously evaluated disaster recovery plan will not only keep an organization going in case of a calamity at the organization's DP facility, but provide the fastest and least expensive way to recovery by having every person act effectively. This applies whether the disaster is caused by external powers or an internal computer criminal.

Hot Site vs. Cold Site

A *hot site* is a fully operational off-site computer facility that is identical with the organization's original computer facility. A hot site is a replica

Contingency and Disaster Recovery Plans

of the organization's computer operations in hardware, software, personnel, and all types of security measures. At the end of each day, a courier takes the tapes of that day's runs from the original computer facility to the hot site so that the latter is never more than one version behind the organization's original computer operations.

A *cold site* is an off-site empty warehouse that offers space for the organization's computer and peripheral equipment in case of a disaster, and provides electric power, air conditioning, fire protection, and possibly security. In case of a disaster, the organization can rent from the manufacturer a compatible hardware, and have it delivered to the cold site. The software usually is taken to this off-site facility once a week from the original DP facility. Quite understandably, the cold site is much cheaper to rent/buy and maintain than the hot site. It also is much less effective in a disaster, resulting in much more damage and financial loss.

10
Hardware Security

The second component in establishing total security for a DP facility or department within a law enforcement or criminal justice agency is hardware security. It consists of the following elements: electric power, biometric ID systems, encryption systems, message authentification system, and voice verification system.

ELECTRIC POWER

Because computer operations are totally dependent on constant and clean electric power, it is imperative to use every possible means to shield the electric power supply from natural disaster or possible sabotage by terrorists. To protect the constant and clean electric power critical to any DP facility, the following measures are recommended:

- An *uninterruptible power supply (UPS) system* is a reliable standby power source. It switches on automatically when there is a deliberate or accidental blackout or brownout, as well as power line anomalies, such as electrical noise and voltage sags—the most frequent cause of system malfunctions and computer errors.

    In the past, UPS, consisting of a rectifier, inverter, and a static switch, was a large equipment that was too bulky and noisy to be located in the computer room. Now most UPS systems are high technology power transistors that are small, quiet, efficient, and can be placed next to the mainframe or minicomputer in the machine room. Moreover, the new transistorized UPS systems are rechargeable, and can generally provide up to 35 or 45 minutes of power to sustain DP operations through a blackout or brownout. And, finally, because these transistorized UPS systems consist of few parts, they hardly need any servicing.

Hardware Security

- An *off-site backup power generator* is another necessary security measure. It is quite expensive, but worth it for large law enforcement agencies because it can save hundreds of thousands of dollars in case of prolonged power failure when there is loss of essential data and transactions of sensitive information. The off-site backup power generator is invaluable in power failure because it switches on automatically before UPS service ends. An emergency power generator provides electric power to the facility's central processing unit so that the computer operations can continue without interruption.

THE TERMINAL—PERSONAL COMPUTER

Without a doubt, the terminal or personal computer or work station—whether local or remote, stand alone, or mainframe-connected, is the most vulnerable device in today's online computer systems. It is the gateway or entrance to all electronic data processing, stored data, and information.

An example is the rash of hackers in recent years, including the three West German men who were part of an Eastern European spy ring. Using their microcomputers the men allegedly broke into key military and research computers in the United States, Europe, and Japan. These individuals allegedly were recruited by the Soviet KGB, and for cash and drugs they supplied the KGB secret and highly sensitive data and information.

But it's not always hackers who use their terminals to break into a computer system. More and more noncomputer employees, so called end users, find their desktop PC a good tool to access confidential or secret information for personal gain or even vendetta. A recent case is the former California Franchise Tax Board employee, Judith Danelle Box. She used (accessed) the state computer—via her terminal—to learn the home addresses of certain Folsom Prison correctional officers targeted for retaliation by members of the feared Aryan Brotherhood prison gang. The 39-year-old Box, who had been a state employee for 19 years, and had no previous police record, accessed and retrieved the data from the Franchise Tax Board computer for her boyfriend, Phillip "Wildman" Fortman, a Folsom Prison inmate and a ranking member of the prison gang.

Because an informer notified the authorities, no assaults were carried out. Nevertheless, Ms. Box was convicted of maliciously gaining access to a state computer, and conspiring to commit an assault with force likely to produce great bodily injury. She was sentenced to three years in prison.

Considering the high risks that terminals and PCs represent, effective hardware security measures against possible unauthorized use of ter-

The Terminal—Personal Computer

minals is imperative. Existing terminal security techniques include: terminal lock and key, magnetic-strip card, biometric ID systems, and transmission security.

Terminal Lock and Key

This is the simplest security measure to use but the easiest to circumvent. The user inserts the correct key into the lock, turns the key, and the system is switched on. If this simple tool is used, the user must understand that he is responsible if anybody gets hold of his key (whether the key is stolen or lost), or makes a copy of the key to be used for theft or abuse of the computer system programs, records, or data.

Magnetic-Strip Card

A magnetic-strip card is more expensive than lock and key, but more effective. The user inserts his private card into a terminal-connected magnetic card reader, and the encoded ID on the card is verified by a control file in the computer system. If the verification is positive, the system switches on. If the verification is negative, the terminal (and the system) remains shut off—it cannot be used.

Employees often are careless with these cards so the company's policy should be to hold the employee responsible if any unauthorized person is accessing sensitive files or data in the computer system via his or her terminal.

Biometric ID Systems

Biometric ID systems are the latest and most efficient hardware security controls against unauthorized accessing of computer systems via terminals or PCs. Biometric ID systems are based on human parameters such as hand geometry, fingerprints, retinal patterns, signature patterns and dynamics, touch patterns, and speech patterns.

Biometric security devices authenticate a person's identity by measuring digitally a physical or behavioral characteristic such as fingerprint, voice inflection, or the pattern of blood vessels in the eye.

Biometric ID systems consist of the following techniques:

- fingerprints and palm prints
- signature analysis
- signature dynamics
- voice prints
- retinal patterns
- touch patterns

Hardware Security

Fingerprint and Palm Prints. For this system the user places his finger or palm on a handshaped electronic pad that is attached to the terminal. The sensors read the finger or palm prints, and match and verify them against stored prints in a control file. If the verification is positive, the system switches on. If the verification is negative, the terminal remains shut off.

Signature Analysis, Signature Dynamics, and Voice Print. These devices, according to some experts, are at least as accurate as finger or palm prints.

- In *signature analysis* the user writes his name on an electronic pad attached to the computer terminal. Next, the signature is compared and verified with stored codes in a control file. If the verification is positive, the system switches on. If the verification is negative, the terminal remains shut off.
- In *signature dynamics* the act of a user signing his name on a terminal-connected electronic pad is measured. That is, the pressure and the velocity of writing is measured electronically, whether it is a full signature or just the initials. If the verification is positive with the stored codes in the system's control file, the system switches on. If the verification is negative, the terminal remains shut off.

  According to experts, signature dynamics is as individual as the minutiae on a person's fingers. It cannot be imitated. In fact, recently a group of researchers in England hired professional forgers and offered them rewards for duplicating other people's signature dynamics. No one was able to collect the large rewards offered.
- With *voice print*, the person speaks certain words into a terminal-attached microphone, and the electronically converted voice message is matched and verified against stored codes in the system's control file. If verification is positive, the system switches on. If verification is negative, the system is inaccessible.

Retinal Patterns. Retinal patterns work when the user looks into a very weak laser device attached to the terminal. The device scans the person's retinal patterns for matching and verification with the codes in the control file. Actually, the user is identified by the pattern of his blood vessels in his eye as it is exposed to the laser device's infrared light. The resulting action by the control file is the same as with the other biometric ID systems.

Touch Patterns. Touch patterns are based on the fact that each person has a unique touch on the terminal's (or for that matter on the typewriter or piano) keyboard. The patterns work when the user keys in his name or any word. As in all the previous techniques of biometric ID systems, the user's touch on the keyboard is matched and verified by stored codes in the system's control file. A positive verification will switch the system on; while a negative verification will leave the terminal shut off.

Fingerprint Security. This is a mixture of biometric ID systems and proximity mode (discussed in chapter 9), and is based on minutiae detection. Specifically, the authorized individual presses his thumb (or some other predetermined finger) upon a small electronic pad near a locked door and the door opens, or a terminal and the system switches on. An intriguing feature of this security is that in case of a dangerous situation, such as a gun pointed against the head by a criminal, the individual simply presses a different finger upon the electronic pad. This sets up an alarm, and the security people can respond immediately.

Transmission Security

Transmission security also is a version of the proximity mode. Transmission security consists of a miniature radio transmitter encased in a thin, hard-shell card. The great advantage of this technique is that the user who has this card in his pocket or wallet can get up and leave his terminal or PC without worrying about shutting off his machine. The transmission security card will shut off his machine automatically when the person is more than a few inches away from his terminal. Subsequently, when he returns and sits down at his terminal, his transmission security card will automatically turn on the machine. Of course, he still will have to key in his ID and password to get back into the computer system.

ENCRYPTION SYSTEMS

Within the last fifteen years two major methods of protecting data security in computer systems and telecommunications have been developed. They are Data Encryption Standard (DES) and Public Key Encryption (PKE). Actually, the only known practical means of deterring possible wiretappers from stealing sensitive data and information transmitted over various communications media is data encryption and decryption.

Data encryption is the precise process or cryptographic algorithm through which the original intelligible data—called *plain text*—is converted to unintelligible sequence of numbers or symbols, called *cipher text*. The reverse process or algorithm through which the cipher text is converted back to plain (intelligible) text is called *data decryption*. Simply put, data encryption is nothing more than scrambling transmitted data so that, if intercepted, they are incomprehensible and consequently useless to the computer criminal; and data decryption unscrambles the transmitted data so that the authorized person receives the original data in understandable form.

Hardware Security

Data Encryption Standard

Recognizing the need to adopt a standard algorithm[1] for the encryption of computer data, the National Bureau of Standards (NBS) put out a Request for Proposal (RFP) for "Cryptographic Algorithm for the Protection of Computer Data During Transmission and Dormant Storage."

Actually, two acts of Congress motivated NBS to search for a standard cryptographic algorithm.[2] The first was the Brooks Act of 1965, giving NBS the "responsibility to create standards which would govern the purchase and use of computers for the Federal Government." (1) The second was the Privacy Act of 1874, "an attempt to keep confidential and secure all data on U.S. citizens in possession of the Government." (2) The Privacy Act (discussed at length in chapter 7) was the result of two major developments: the availability of inexpensive electronic devices to intercept sensitive, confidential, and secret data, and the increasing number of geographical distributed computer systems dependent upon telecommunications.

The NBS request for proposal listed the following requirements for an acceptable encryption algorithm:

- It must be specific and unambiguous
- It must have methods of protection based only on the secrecy of the keys
- It must not discriminate against any user or supplier

On July 15, 1977, after NBS accepted the IBM-designed cryptographic algorithm, the federal government officially adopted IBM's DES. In 1980, the American National Standards Institution (ANSI) adopted it for commercial use.

DES uses what is called the *private key approach*. This approach consists of a single secret conversion key that encrypts data sent over public channels such as cable, microwave, fiberoptics, and satellite, in addition to the DES' cryptographic algorithm or cipher system. The same single key is relayed to the authorized receiver over a secured channel such as unlisted, private telephone, or sent by a courier. Subsequently, the

---

[1] A simple algorithm is a set of well-defined rules and procedures for the solution of a problem in a finite number of steps. Examples include a computer program, a flowchart/decision table, a Warnier-Orr diagram, and a risk analysis.

[2] A cryptographic algorithm is a definitive set of computational procedures that resolves a problem or performs a mathematical transformation within a finite number of structured steps and a *key* (password or code) to transfer/convert intelligible text to unintelligible or scrambled text and vice versa. And a key/password/code is a specific combination or pattern of characters or bits (binary digits) that serves as a secret parameter or sequence of numbers used in a given cryptographic algorithm.

Encryption Systems

receiver decrypts the data. As soon as a person inputs or sends data over a telecommunication system—if the facility uses DES—the data is encrypted, that is, scrambled. Only when the targeted person receives from the sender the secret key or password, can he decrypt or unscramble the data (FIG. 10-1).

The DES key consists of 64 bits or characters—56 bits for the key/password, and 8 bits for error detection. The DES algorithm encrypts a block of 64 bits at one time. DES is considered secure because it has a strong cryptographic algorithm, coupled with an *S-box* (switch-box) the hardware (encryptor) that implements it; uses block encryption to convert a stream of input bits of fixed length plain (intelligible) text into a fixed length but different cipher (scrambled) text. Cryptography experts believe that because there are 72 quadrillion possible keys (combination of passwords or codes) to use in DES it would take a hundred years or so for a cryptanalyst[3] to break it. However, the security of DES is dependent upon the security of the 64 bits key. No encryption system is stronger than the protection given to the key or keys.

Public Key Encryption

Because there was controversy in NBS choosing the IBM's algorithm for DES, Martin E. Hellman and Whitfield Diffie proposed the development of a public key encryption in November 1976. Hellman and Diffie claimed that with their public key encryption method they would solve the problems they found with DES. They would be able to maintain the secrecy of a transmitted key, and meet the requirements of message authentification.

Hellman and Diffie's proposed concept became known as the PKE (FIG. 10-2) or public key approach. PKE's cryptographic algorithm is quite different from the cryptographic algorithm of DES. The main concept of

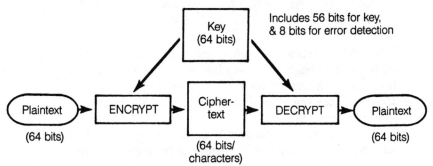

Fig. 10-1. Data encryption standard.

---

[3]A perpetrator who penetrates or breaks into an encryption system is known as a cryptanalyst.

Hardware Security

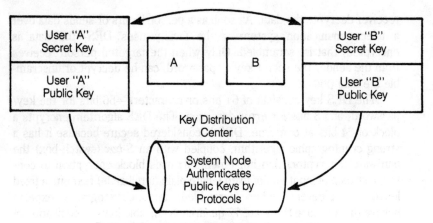

Fig. 10-2. Public key encryption standard.

PKE is that it consists of two separate keys or passwords that are essential in the encryption and decryption of data. Each user—both sender and receiver—has two keys: one public key and one secret key. Or putting it another way, each user has an encryption (public) key, and a decryption (secret) key.

The PKE encryption system works like this:

- User "A transmits his public key and the public key of user "B" to system node (key distribution center), or vice versa. (The public keys of all users are registered and stored in the system node.)
- After both public keys are authenticated by protocols—verified that the transmitted keys are registered and stored—the system node notifies user "B" that user "A" wishes to communicate.
  User "B" acknowledges the communication, that is, through system node he lets user "A" know that he is ready to receive data.
- User "A" encrypts his data/message using his secret key, and transmits it to user "B." His plain text is converted into cipher text, and is transmitted via fiberoptics, or satellite.
- User "A" then sends his secret key to user "B" by bonded courier or unlisted telephone.
- User "B," upon receiving user "A's" secret key, can decrypt the data/message appearing on the screen of his computer terminal.

There are many versions of PKE and just as many different cryptographic algorithms used. An example of the many PKEs is the *key management system* that uses the RSA cryptographic algorithm named after its inventors: River, Shamir, and Adleman. In Key Management System a certain number of users can communicate with each other at the same time, provided they have the other persons' secret and public keys, and they agree on the time of communication.

MESSAGE AUTHENTIFICATION CODE

The Message Authentification Code (MAC) technique, which consists of having cryptographic check digits appended to electronic message, is a valuable tool for criminal justice and law enforcement officials. MAC check digits refer to the transaction type, point of origin and destination of the message, and other identification information. Messages without such additional check digits are rejected by the receiving agency. Of course, the receiving agency must have a MAC with their encryption system. In other words, both sending and receiving agencies must have MAC to be able to communicate.

MAC, in conjunction with DES or PKE, is best utilized when it is implemented within a hardware security module. The module can be self-contained, physically secure, microprocessor-controlled, and security device programmed to perform all the cryptographic functions. The module can be a data processing peripheral device that interfaces with the organization's computer system(s). The interfacing can be accomplished by the computer sending sensitive data or information directly to the module to perform its functions.

By this method, the information sent—as well as the keys or passwords used in encrypting the information—is never in the open. Moreover, the hardware module can be secured by both physical locks and interlock circuitry, so that all the information that has to be transformed from plain text to cipher text is within the module. Additionally, no matter how this module is opened—whether legitimately by two physical keys entrusted to two people or forced open—the built-in interlock circuitry causes all data stored in the module, as well as the cryptographic algorithm and the keys or passwords, to be erased. (Something like the devices seen on *Mission Impossible*.) This is the kind of security that the FBI can use in connection with certain highly sensitive NCIC files.

VOICE VERIFICATION SYSTEM

This system identifies users by recognizing basic phonetic patterns. The system, using a word-recognition algorithm, works on isolated words instead of continuous speech. It randomly selects four words for the user to say, and the user has four chances to respond correctly.

If the response is correct and the user's voice is verified in the control file, the system is turned on. If the user's response is correct but his voice is unverifiable, or if his response is incorrect, he is unable to access the computer system even if his terminal is switched on.

11

Software Security

The third component in effecting sound electronic data processing security is software security. An efficient software security is imperative as a preventive measure, whether the law enforcement or criminal justice agency is large, medium, or small.

Software security is comprised of the following measures.

SOFTWARE PROTECTION LEVELS

It is the top law enforcement official's responsibility to determine which software is to be protected and at what security level. This decision should be based on risk and cost/benefit analyses. The higher risk the software is exposed to, the higher security level it should be accorded. Conversely, the more stringent security is given to the particular software, the more it will cost. Budget considerations are always part of such management decisions.

AGENCY SECURITY POLICY AND CONTROL PROCEDURES

To deter computer crime and prevent the theft, abuse, or sabotage of the law enforcement or criminal justice agency's software, a clear and concise computer security policy and control procedures should be published and distributed to the departments and rigorously enforced. For example, each person who uses a terminal or PC must understand that unauthorized use of the department's computer systems and programs is prohibited. This includes using the computer for playing games; for private business, such as preparing personal income tax, or balancing financial statements; for copying a program, or giving certain information from a record to an outsider.

Software Security

A well-written Security Policy and Control Procedures Manual should make it absolutely clear that first-time offenders will be reprimanded; that second-time offenders will be put on probation; and that third-time offenders will be terminated. (That is, if such is the top official's defined policy.) The manual also should state that if any law enforcement DP staff or user is found adding, deleting, or changing any records, files, or programs for the purpose of some illegal activity, he or she will face the maximum disciplinary action.

Of course, if the agency does not rigorously enforce its written computer security policy, such a document then is just an exercise in futility. In other words, if the agency is satisfied only to terminate the offender without filing criminal charges, the best security manual is a waste of effort.

SOFTWARE PROTECTION/ SOFTWARE CONTROL SYSTEMS

There are many excellent software security/software control packages on the market, but because of space only a few are mentioned here. They include ACF 2, developed by SKK, Inc., and marketed by Cambridge Systems Group; Top Secret, developed by CGA Software Products Group, Inc.; and Resource Access Control Facility (RACF), developed and marketed by IBM.

RACF, a comprehensive software security product for large computer systems such as the FBI and the Department of Justice operates, protects, and monitors systems via the following features:

- It controls access to the system by identifying and verifying the users before they log on. It establishes user identity prior to allowing access to protected resources through its user profile feature. Each user's profile is made up of name, userid, group name (which department or subdepartment the user belongs to), password, last changed (date when new password was given), and attributes. RACF performs its major functions by building profiles as to who is allowed to use what and how at the facility, based on information input into RACF at the time this software application is implemented, and as new users get on the organization's computer system.

    These profiles, which reside on RACF datasets, contain descriptions of each user and the group he belongs to (who); each resource in the system (what); and the level of authorization (how).

    RACF also has a terminal profile for each PC or work station in the organization, ensuring that only staff authorized to particular terminals are using it. And RACF has dataset profile for all sensi-

Software Protection/Software Control Systems

tive records to ensure that only authorized persons can access those particular datasets or records.

Furthermore, RACF authenticates the users by verifying that they are who they say they are. Only users with the proper level of authorization can access particular records and data. Moreover, RACF delegates only the level of authorization that is needed and defined on RACF datasets for the particular users.

- It monitors the system by logging detected unauthorized attempts and detected actual accesses to sensitive data or information. RACF provides immediate notification of abnormal situations at the operator console in the machine room and alerts computer security personnel about access violations via exception or security reports. It is possible for RACF to monitor unauthorized attempts and actual accesses because when a user logs on to the computer system, if he does not have the proper password, he is given three chances to try again. After three chances, the terminal will switch off without letting the person access the system and RACF will immediately notify the operator console, as well as report the incident in an exception report to the proper authorities.

Simply put, RACF limits access to an agency's sensitive software through its highly structured profile features. Specifically, RACF controls that only authorized staff can use the system, and that only users with proper level of authorization can access confidential or secret records and data. (See FIG. 11-1 for an overview of RACF.)

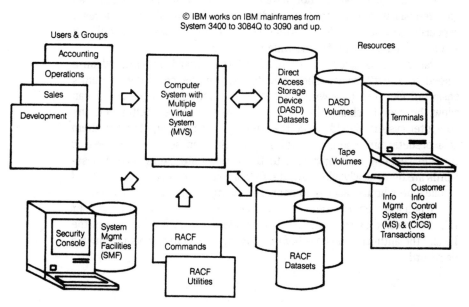

Fig. 11-1. Overview of Resource Access Control Facility (RACF).

113

Software Security

For some law enforcement agencies, a data dictionary that protects the accessing of software is more appropriate. For example, The Repository, a sophisticated data dictionary system developed by IBM, is more appropriate and affordable than most software control systems. There are many other inexpensive software protection application packages on the market that law enforcement agencies on a tight budget can utilize.

SYSTEMS AND PROGRAMMING STANDARDS

Establishing systems and programming standards is essential for software security. By defining, for example, naming conventions for systems and programs, and for data elements and datasets, and establishing uniformity for the length and meaning of all the above names, they facilitate overall controls. For example, in systems naming conventions one might establish the standards that the first four positions are reserved for the particular system's ID, such as CJIS for Criminal Justice Information System or NCIC for National Crime Information Center. While in program naming conventions one might establish the standards that one position is reserved to show the sex of the suspect, such as "1" for Male, "2" for Female, and "3" for unknown.

PASSWORD SECURITY

For agencies that do not have a software protection system, an encoded password is the first line of defense against unauthorized access, especially in online systems. Moreover, reusable passwords should be eliminated and replaced by one-time passwords.

Passwords for access authorization levels should be allocated on a "need to know" basis. They can be kept in the computer system's password file. The password file can be one-way encrypted, and it can allow the user to change his or her password anytime. Better yet, the computer system should create the passwords at random, changing them at a predetermined interval, and sending them in sealed envelopes or through secured electronic mail to the appropriate users. When passwords are dynamically allocated, the risk of a staff stealing the password of a colleague who has access to sensitive records is greatly diminished.

When a law enforcement staff member enters his password and user ID, it is verified by the system's control file. The verification covers the ID and the authorization level before allowing access to any data in any file or record.

APPLICATIONS CONTROLS

Applications controls designed into individual programs is another critical software crime deterrence measure. Typical applications controls include: input, processing, change, testing, and output controls.

- *Input controls*, if properly designed, ensure that each transaction is entered correctly, and only once, and that only authorized transactions enter the computer system.
- *Processing controls* verify that the transactions entered into the system are processed against the proper files; that each component of each transaction is valid; and that any invalid transaction rejected by the system is reentered correctly.
- *Change controls* are essential for maintaining standard procedures in system and program modifications, and for safeguarding the integrity of the system. Change controls serves as an effective deterrent against the potential embezzler or disgruntled employee bent on sabotaging the organization's computer systems.
- *Test controls* ensure that the system, application, and/or program work efficiently separately and together before the system is going into the production mode.
- *Output controls* authenticate all the previous controls by repeating the functions of input and processing. Such repetitive activities help to ensure that only authorized and accurate transactions are processed.

12

Personnel Security

The fourth and final component of a sound and comprehensive computer security strategy is personnel security. In fact, a strong, constructive personnel policy that is based on affirmative management philosophy can provide a powerful deterrence against computer crime.

Having said that, it must be admitted that sophisticated physical, hardware, and software monitoring systems, security guards, effective access control techniques, and systems and applications controls, and encryption systems, make it more difficult for a potential computer criminal to steal or copy data, embezzle, sell confidential information, steal CPU time, use programs and applications covertly for material gains, or sabotage the system.

But it is not enough! Unless there is a definitive and enforceable personnel security policy that covers rules of conduct and employment life cycle from hiring, continued education, performance evaluation, promotion, mandatory annual vacation, and termination, no maximum or even minimum computer security can be achieved in any law enforcement or criminal justice agency that operates an automated crime information system.

Besides, a realistic risk analysis in any data processing environment is not complete unless it includes personnel security risks. These risks must take into consideration every staff who is using the computer system.

BACKGROUND INVESTIGATION

All job applicants must be thoroughly screened. This applies not only to criminal justice and law enforcement agencies who routinely do background investigation of a job applicant before he can take a written examination, but federal, state, and local agencies as well.

Personnel Security

It is not an invasion of privacy to have the applicant's work references, school records, driving records, and possible criminal records investigated.

PERSONNEL FOLLOW UP

A thorough background screening of a job applicant will possibly—but not absolutely—eliminate a person with a shady past. There must be an affirmative personnel follow up ensuring that the employee will get a periodic objective performance evaluation, an opportunity to further his education and hone his skills, and will be considered for promotion. Without such affirmative personnel follow up, there is always the probability that an employee (without any prior criminal record) will become disgruntled—and disgruntlement very often results in a computer crime.

In addition, an affirmative personnel policy will maintain high employee morale and a productive staff.

One of the more effective strategies for job satisfaction is the *cognitive style positioning*. The system (quite interestingly, is also used by the FBI for criminal profiling) shows that people approach assignments/projects, situations, problems, and problem solving differently.

It was found that people can be categorized within the following four defined cognitive styles:

- *The analyzer* or the analytical person approaches assignments and problems by carefully examining and analyzing all the facts before recommending any solution.
- *The evaluator* or the pragmatic person approaches assignments and problems in an objective, precise manner. His solution to a problem is pragmatic.
- *The conceptualizer* or the creative person approaches his assignments and problems creatively. He recommends a solution after seeing the whole picture of the situation.
- *The energizer* or the communicator can understand the viewpoint of both the technical/law enforcement professionals and the nontechnical users. His approach to assignments and solving of problems relies on good communications.

According to this concept, if the employees' cognitive styles are determined, it is up to the supervisor to position or organize each project, each assignment, so that it includes at least one representative of each cognitive style. Because different cognitive style people work well together as a team, the chances are better that the project—whether it's a stake-out, a sting operation, or a drug-bust—will be well done. More

A Checklist for Defining the Different Types of Cognitive Style

importantly, this concept—when carried out well—makes for job satisfaction, the most potent antidote against computer-aided crime.

A CHECKLIST FOR DEFINING THE DIFFERENT TYPES OF COGNITIVE STYLE

The Analyzer

- Is the person handling every decision, every assignment, every problem deliberately, analyzing every aspect of the matter?
- When he or she gives an opinion or makes a statement, is it based on fact and sound logic?
- Can he or she be relied upon not to act or react impulsively?
- Is his or her handwriting neat and trim? Are the i's dotted and the t's crossed with a decisive stroke? Is this signature large and strong?

These behavior characteristics indicate an *analyzer* type of cognitive style.

The Evaluator

- Is he or she dealing with assignments, problems, and decisions in an objective, almost detached, precise manner?
- Can he or she be relied upon to observe all the rules and regulations of the organization?
- Is he or she very careful, even pedantic in written and oral communications?
- Is his or her handwriting painfully neat? Are all i's dotted and t's crossed very carefully? Is his or her signature rather plain, without any flair?

These behavior characteristics indicate an *evaluator* type of cognitive style.

The Conceptualizer

- Is the individual approaching assignments and problems, as well as decisions, creatively?
- Is his or her creativity at times too much? That is, does he or she often come up with a "brilliant idea" to change something when the project is halfway finished? Because of such "flashes" does he or she then create more work for his colleagues and effect cost overrun for the project?
- Is his or her handwriting large and all over the page? Are very few i's dotted and t's crossed? Is his or her signature artistic, unique, and almost impossible to read?

Personnel Security

These behavior characteristics indicate an *conceptualizer* type of cognitive style.

The Energizer

- Is he or she by knowledge, temperament, and political acumen a perfect liaison between all levels and types of law enforcement and criminal justice practitioners?
- Is he or she an excellent communicator?
- To be on good terms with all concerned, does he or she "agree" with both parties, even if that means more work and problems even for colleagues?
- Is his or her handwriting round and almost too nice? Are all a's and o's closed with many of them showing a "hook"? Is his or her signature rather variable? In other words, is the way he or she signs his or her name inconsistent?

These behavior characteristics indicate an *energizer* type of cognitive style.

By responding to this checklist, one can draw a pretty accurate profile of any individual in the workplace. Based upon this analysis, a team can be set up to include a combination of cognitive styles to achieve better performance, have projects completed on time, and perhaps most importantly, effect an *esprit de corps*.

POSSIBLE INDICTORS OF DISCONTENTMENT

Symptoms that might indicate a disgruntled staff, and symptoms that a supervisor will want to investigate expeditiously in a low-key manner include the following:

- Excessive absenteeism or unwarranted overtime
- Persistent late arrival for work
- Sudden low-quality, low-production output
- Complaints or grumblings to colleagues always to fellow employees; never to the supervisor directly
- Putting off vacation

Any or all of these symptoms might indicate job frustration or job stress and not disgruntlement. However, a good supervisor knows that such things are often the catalysts for computer-aided crime, and will not ignore any such signs. The supervisor will look into any possible problem by communicating with the person on a one-to-one basis in private.

By talking to the employee as soon as possible, the supervisor might be able to minimize, if not completely eliminate, the reason for any employee dissatisfaction and eliminate possible security threat to the sensitive data processed and stored at the agency.

SEPARATION OF DUTIES OF COMPUTER STAFF

It is essential that separation of duties and responsibilities of employees is established in a law enforcement data processing department. Specifically, employees who prepare source documents are not to enter data into the computer system and perform verification. Data entry operators in batch processing, for example, are to be divided into two groups: the first group is to enter the data into the terminals, and the second group is to verify that the input data is accurate before the data is to be processed.

Similarly, the police programmer who codes, tests, and debugs the programs in a new or modified system is not to be the person who tests the completed programs in the system tests. The reason is twofold:

- The programmer usually is proud of his creation. Consequently, consciously or unconsciously, he does not want to find anything wrong with his programs, and so he will overlook inconsequential bugs. Inconsequential bugs have a way of becoming big trouble and cause systems to malfunction.
- The systems analyst and the users can verify via the systems test that the programs respond to their requirements.

The data processing employee whose duty is to reconcile batch totals, for example, is not to be the same person who either prepares the batch tools, or the person who inputs the data for processing from source documents.

The principle in all the separation of duties of data processing staff is the same as in the business world: The person who prepares checks or drafts is never the same person who signs the checks.

PROPER SECURITY ORIENTATION FOR NEW OFFICERS

Proper security orientation is mandatory to impress upon new staff the importance of security relating to every phase of work in a data processing facility, including the necessity of having controlled access to machine rooms, labs, and copying machines. Security orientation should be followed by periodic seminars on security given by knowledgeable security professionals who are good communicators.

Personnel Security

ENFORCING SECURITY POLICIES

It's extremely important that security policies are enforced. For example, it must be communicated to every data processing and nondata processing officer at every level that discussion of sensitive information (passwords, data in the databases, and the like) outside the department could be grounds for dismissal. Every law enforcement and criminal justice practitioner must be made aware that the agency has established and is enforcing strict procedures for any type of employment termination.

The termination procedures is to include: handing a severance check to the (voluntarily or involuntarily) terminated employee; asking for the person's magnetic strip card or proximity mode card; physically escorting the person out of the building; erasing immediately the person's password in the computer system; and giving instructions to the guards in the lobby to never allow that person back into the facility. Never allow the person—even if he is resigning and not terminated—to stay there two weeks. As several case histories have proven, such employees can destroy invaluable data by inserting a time bomb or a virus or a worm into the computer system during the two-week period. To avoid any such possibility, the moment he submits his resignation, he is to be given a severance paycheck and escorted from the building by security officers.

Appendix A

Western Identification Network, Inc.

Western Identification Network (WIN), a multistate automated fingerprint identification system, became fully operational in November 1989 in Alaska, California, Idaho, Nevada, Oregon, Utah, Washington, Wyoming, and the Portland Police Bureau. One of the benefits that these and the three remaining Western States—Arizona, Colorado, and Montana—hope to achieve by having a multistate AFIS is the capability to search criminal data in multiple states.

Although WIN's host computer system is physically located in Sacramento, California, remote input stations (RISs) and booking terminals have been installed at various agencies in the participating states.

WIN has proven that its database is capable of processing 18,000 arrest cards and 3,400 crime scene latent prints per month against 1.4 million criminal fingerprint records.

During the first six weeks of processing, law enforcement agencies using WIN made 231 tenprint identifications, which resulted in 29 criminals being served with outstanding warrants. Also, numerous identifications involved out-of-state cards. One of the more resourceful criminals was identified by four separate records: two in Oregon, and two in Utah.

During the first five weeks of WIN operation, the Portland Police Bureau made 63 latent hits, which resulted in a total of 109 identifications. One suspect, after being identified by WIN AFIS, was linked to 20 additional cases.

The multistate concept worked well for Wyoming. Forty-two out of the state's 70 tenprint hits were from neighboring states—a 60% out-of-state hit rate.

Appendix A

One of the features of the WIN database architecture is its *scar pattern search*. Specifically, the database design requires each inquiry to search all records with scar pattern types. One-tenth of one percent of the database is allocated to scar patterns (one scar per 100 cards). As the percentage of scars exceeds this amount, response time and throughput suffer accordingly. Therefore, all WIN users are asked to keep the use of scar pattern types to a minimum.

Recently it has been proposed that WIN and National Law Enforcement Telecommunication System (NLETS) combine resources by sharing dedicated telephone lines. Alaska line is being considered first. Under this configuration, WIN would run a line to Phoenix; NLETS would double the speed of their Alaska line, then multiplex it: half for NLETS and half for WIN.

Because of the high cost of communications—currently over $10,000 a month—WIN's administration is looking into the feasibility of the NEC developing a dial-up software for AFIS. Thus, the money currently being paid to AT&T could then be directed to NEC for AFIS enhancements.

WIN WORK LOAD STATISTICS

The following information is based on WIN Activity Reports received since WIN implementation:

Tenprint Processing

Tenprint Inquiries	35,779
Tenprint Identifications	2,488
Hit Rate	7%
Tenprint Registrations	29,162

Latent Print Processing

Latent Print Inquiries	2,209
Latent Print Identifications	248
Hit Rate	11.2%

Latent Print Identifications—Crime Types

Burglary	173
Drugs	9
Homicide	8
Rape/Kidnap	2
Robbery	8
Auto Theft	4
Forgery	1

Appendix B
Direct Electronic Fingerprinting (Lifescan)

Until recently, ink-produced fingerprint images (FIG. B-1), which were originated in the early 1900s, was the accepted method of positively identifying individuals in the criminal justice community. Ink fingerprint impressions, however, often had to be rejected because:

- Too much ink was used, causing smudge
- Insufficient ink was used, causing ridge characteristics to be unclear
- The entire first joint of each finger was not completely inked and rolled

The deficiencies often made it impossible for manual fingerprint classification and searching, as well as difficult for automated fingerprint scanning by the automated fingerprint identification system (AFIS).

DEF

As a response to the need to have a more efficient method of fingerprint imaging to enhance and thus utilize the high technology of AFIS, direct electronic fingerprinting (DEF) was developed (FIG. B-2). In the simplest of terms, DEF is the electronic scanning of an individual's fingers. The scan is then processed, displayed on the computer screen for the technician's approval, and then printed out locally and/or transmitted to a central site. At the central site, a tenprint card is printed and the fingerprint image is entered into AFIS for searching and matching purposes.

Appendix B

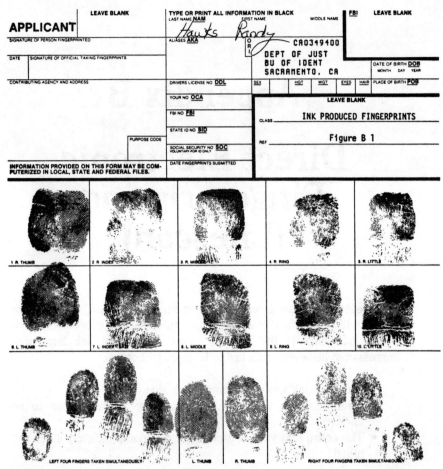

Fig. B-1. Ink-produced fingerprints (Lifescan).

Because the DEF process involves electronic scanning of fingers instead of ink, this technology provides the following advantages over the ink fingerprint impressions:

- No more smudged prints
- No ink-stained hands
- High contrast, black and white images
  - Truer automated minutiae detection
  - Improved automated search process
  - Improved quality of records in the AFIS database
- Immediate technician feedback which allows a specific finger to be retaken, instead of the entire card

Direct Electronic Fingerprinting

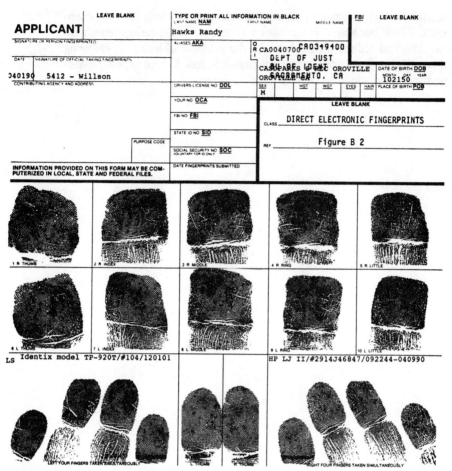

Fig. B-2. Direct electronic fingerprints.

- Multiple, identical copies from one reading on selected formats to state, FBI, or a specific agency
- Future computer tape or direct transmission to the state and/or FBI

To appreciate DEF, one needs to understand how image transmission works. The basic process in image transmission is compression of data prior to transmission, and decompression of data after transmission. The method of compression and decompression works well for printed text and ordinary photographs. However, minute details are lost or changed when using this technique with fingerprint images that necessitate the

Appendix B

transmission and printing of the captured fingerprints in binary representation. Thus, because a compression algorithm would reduce transmission time and reduce if not eliminate the problem of losing or changing minute data in fingerprint image transmission, this feature is being developed and to be added to DEF in the near future.

Glossary

ACHS Abbreviation for Automated Criminal History System, a subsystem of most states' computerized Criminal Justice Information System.

acquittal Judgment of a court stating that the defendant is not guilty of the offense(s) for which he was tried. Acquittal is based on either the verdict of a jury or a judicial officer.

adult A person 18 years of age or older.

AIS Abbreviation for Automated Identification System, a subsystem of the FBI's National Crime Information System.

ALVS Abbreviation for Automated Locating Vehicle System, a computer application for law enforcement in the field.

appeal A petition initiated by the defendant for a rehearing in an appellate court as to a previous sentence or motion.

arrest ". . . Taking a person into custody, in a case and in the manner authorized by law. An arrest may be made by a peace officer or by a private person." (P.C. 834).

article Stolen property, such as a television, camera, power tool, etc., that has a serial number or owner-applied number and does not meet the entry criteria for any other NCIC property database such as Stolen Vehicle database, Stolen Boat database, etc.

artificial intelligence A field of study generally concerned with making computer systems imitate human thinking. Research in artificial intelligence has resulted in robotics, expert systems, and many other new concepts.

biometric ID systems An array of the latest and most effective electronic computer security techniques to deter a person from accessing records and sensitive information in Automated Crime Information Systems.

CAD Abbreviation for Computer-Aided Dispatch, a computer application for the law enforcement officer in a patrol car. The officer can

Glossary

access the available criminal justice systems' databases directly without having to go through the local police dispatcher.

CAL-ID Abbreviation for California Automated Fingerprint Identification System operated by the California Department of Justice in Sacramento, CA.

CAMEO Abbreviation for Computer-Aided Management of Emergency Operations, an application to assist law enforcement agencies.

charge a formal allegation that a specific person has committed a specific offense.

CJIS Abbreviation for Criminal Justice Information System, a computer system that most states have to keep track of the criminal activities within its own border.

clearance An offense is cleared or solved for crime reporting purposes when at least one person is arrested, charged with the commission of the offense, and turned over to the court for prosecution.

CLETS Abbreviation for California Law Enforcement Telecommunications System, operated by the California Department of Justice in Sacramento, CA.

controlled substance A drug substance, or immediate precursor which is included in Schedule I through V inclusive, as set forth in Health and Safety Code Section 11054 through 11058. Controlled substances include heroin, marijuana, amphetamines, barbiturates, and psychedelics.

conviction A judgment (based on either the verdict of a jury or a judicial officer or on the guilty plea of the defendant) stating that the defendant is guilty.

court An agency of the judicial branch of the government, authorized or established by statute or constitution, having one or more judicial officers on its staff. A court has the authority to decide upon controversies in law and disputed matters of fact brought before it.

crime "... An act committed or omitted in violation of a law forbidding or commanding it ..." (P.C. 15).

defendant A person against whom a criminal proceeding is pending.

determinate sentencing Sentencing that by law requires imposition of a term of imprisonment proportionate to the seriousness of the crime, with sentences uniform for like crimes.

dismissal A decision by a judicial officer to terminate a case without a determination of guilt or innocence (see nolo contendere).

disposition, court An action taken as the result of an appearance in court by a defendant. The disposition of a case can range from dismissal or acquittal, to conviction and sentencing of the defendant.

disposition, police An action taken as the result of an arrest. Disposition can range from the offender being released by a law enforcement

Glossary

officer, to being referred to another jurisdiction, to formal misdemeanor or felony complaint being sought via the district attorney.

disposition, prosecutor An action taken as the result of complaints that were requested by the arresting law enforcement agency. Such disposition can range from the prosecutor granting the misdemeanor or felony complaint, to denying the complaint because of lack of probable cause, interest of justice, victim declining to prosecute, or illegal search and seizure by law enforcement.

DNA Abbreviation for deoxyribonucleic acid, the genetic code that many people call the genetic fingerprint because it is equal to or perhaps even more reliable and definitive than the traditional fingerprint in identifying a person

exclusionary rule 1. Evidence gained by law enforcement officers in violation of the 4th Amendment of the U.S. Constitution is inadmissible in a trial. 2. A witness may not testify as to intent or state of mind of another person.

expert systems Computer systems, based on artificial intelligence, that are given basic knowledge about a particular subject and the rules of thumb that an expert in that field would employ to make decisions using that knowledge. Based on that input, the specially designed computer systems are able to solve particular problems just as human experts would.

felony "... A crime which is punishable with death or by imprisonment in the State prison ..." (P.C. 17).

Henry system A manual fingerprint matching and identification process that has been used for centuries. This system was named after Sir Edward Henry. The Henry System assigns an alphanumeric code or "primary" to each finger. Subsequently, the fingerprints are sorted and stored by age, sex, and primary.

indictment A formal, written accusation charging one or more persons with the commission of a crime, and presented by a grand jury to the superior court when the jury has found, after examining the presented evidence, that there is a valid case.

INLETS Abbreviation for International Law Enforcement Telecommunications System, operated by Scotland Yard in London, and connected to INTERPOLE, the International Police Agency.

latent print A fingerprint left behind in a crime scene by an unknown suspect without a clue as to its owner's sex, age, or race.

lower court Municipal or justice court.

Glossary

minutiae Fingerprint characteristics such as lines, swirls, and points at the end of a finger that can be scanned by a computer. Points of minutiae, contrary to the manual Henry System, can be read, entered, and matched in automated fingerprint identification systems such as CAL-ID.

misdemeanor A crime punishable by imprisonment in the county jail, by a fine, or by both. Under certain conditions, as defined by Section 17 of the penal code, a felony crime can be treated as a misdemeanor.

NCIC Abbreviation for National Crime Information Center, the largest Automated Crime Information System in the country. It is operated by the FBI in Washington.

NLETS Abbreviation for National Law Enforcement Telecommunications System, used by law enforcement agencies across the country for accessing Automated Crime Information Systems such as NCIC. NLETS is located in Phoenix, Arizona.

nolo contendere An agreement by a defendant to accept the punishment for an alleged offense, while not directly admitting guilt.

OBTS Abbreviation for Offender-Based Transaction Statistics, a system designed to collect statistical information on the various processes within the criminal justice system that occur between point of arrest and point of final disposition.

parole An added period of control, following completion of the determinate sentence. (P.C. 300(a)).

penal code Abbreviation P.C., a set of laws governing criminal actions, as mandated by a state or a country.

PC Abbreviation for personal computer, a microcomputer

plain view doctrine A legal concept that allows evidence seized by law enforcement without a warrant as admissible, if such evidence was in "plain view;" that is, if the evidence could be seen plainly, such as through the window of an automobile stopped for a traffic violation.

prison A state correctional facility where a person is confined following conviction of a felony offense.

probable cause 1. The minimum level of evidence needed to make a lawful arrest or obtain a specific warrant. 2. The minimum level of information that would provide a prudent law enforcement officer to believe that a crime was being or had been committed by a person(s) to warrant arrest.

probation A judicial requirement that a person fulfill certain conditions of behavior in lieu of a sentence to confinement, but sometime including a jail sentence.

Glossary

prosecutor An attorney employed by a government agency whose official duty is to initiate and maintain criminal proceedings on behalf of the government against a person accused of committing criminal offenses.

proximity mode Electronic equipment used against unauthorized entry into a sensitive area of Automated Crime Information Systems of law enforcement, or any other computer facility.

removal A case removed from the active caseload and no longer under the supervision of the probation department, or a case not removed but escalated to a more advanced level of supervision.

superior court The court of original or trial jurisdiction for felony cases. Also the first court of appeal for municipal or justice court cases.

trial A determination of guilt or innocence by a judge, jury, or by the court on the basis of testimony contained in a transcript.

triple I Abbreviation for Interstate Identification Index, a subsystem of FBI's NCIC.

UPS Abbreviation for Uninterruptible Power Supply, an essential part of any computer system, because without continuous, clean electricity no computer system can function.

UCAN Abbreviation for United Crime Alert Network, a computer application that links local law enforcement officials and merchants to minimize the passing of bad or bogus checks or credit cards.

wheels Fleet management system, a computer application used by law enforcement.

WIN Abbreviation for Western Identification Network, a network of computers with networking capabilities that provide fast and accurate fingerprint information to the twelve western states that are members of WIN.

WSIN Abbreviation for Western States Information Network, a computer system that is used by the western states for information on drug dealers, smugglers, and anything connected to the drug scene.

Bibliography

"A Future In Crime for DNA," *The Sacramento Bee*, August 1988.
"A Better Fingerprint, DNA," *U.S. News & World Report*, July 1988.
"Automated Fingerprint Identification Systems: Technology and Policy Issues," U.S. Department of Justice, Bureau of Justice Statistics, NCJ-104342, April 1987.
Bishop, Demery, R., and Timothy J. Schuessler. "The National Crime Information Center's Missing Person File," *The FBI Law Enforcement Bulletin*, August 1982.
"CAL-ID, California Identification System," California Department of Justice, April 1984.
"California Justice Information System (CJIS)," California Department of Justice, September 1988.
"California Law Enforcement Telecommunications System (CLETS)," California Department of Justice, August 1981.
California Identification System (CAL-ID) and Remote Access Network (RAN), Status Report," California Department of Justice, Calendar Year 1987.
Carlson, Kenneth, and Jan Chaiken. "White Collar Crime," U.S. Department of Justice, Bureau of Justice Statistics, Special Report, September 1987.
Carroll, John M. *Interfacing Thought: Cognitive Aspects of Human-Computer Interaction*, MIT Press, 1987.
"Computerized Criminal History Program," Ibid, March 1984.
"Crime and Fingerprints," *Los Angeles Times*, October 1985.
"Criminal History Inquiry Manual," California Department of Justice, Bureau of Criminal Identification, December 1984.
"Cornell Delays Release of Virus Report," *ComputerWorld*, March 1989.
Cunningham, William C., and Todd H. Taylor. "The Growing Role of Private Security," U.S. Department of Justice, National Institute of Justice, Research Brief, October 1984.
Deoxyribonucleic Acid (DNA), Genetic Clues Add to Crime Solving," United Press International, May 21, 1988.
"DNA Helps Catch Killer," *London Times*, January 16, 1988.

Bibliography

Douglas, John E., and Alan E. Burgess. "Criminal Profiling," FBI Law Enforcement Bulletin, December 1986, pp 9-13.
FBI Law Enforcement Bulletin, August 1985, Vol. 54, p. 8.
FBI Law Enforcement Bulletin, December 1986, Vol. 55, p. 12.
"Electronic Sleuths," *The Wall Street Journal*, November 8, 1984.
Geller, William. American Bar Foundation. "Deadly Force," U.S. Department of Justice, National Institute of Justice, March 1987.
Herrnstein, Richard. Harvard University, "Biology and Crime," U.S. Department of Justice, National Institute of Justice, June 1987.
Hoffman, Peter. U.S. Parole Commission. "Predicting Criminality," U.S. Department of Justice, National Institute of Justice, May 1986.
Icove, David J. "Automated Crime Profiling," FBI Law Enforcement Bulletin, December 1986, pp. 27-30.
James, Fred. "New Fingerprint ID Enhancement," Government Technology, July/August 1988.
Kalish, Carol B. "International Crime Rates," U.S. Department of Justice, Bureau of Justice Statistics, Special Report, May 1988.
Kaplan, John. Stanford University. "Heroin," U.S. Department of Justice, National Institute of Justice, February 1985.
Kelling, George L., Robert Wasserman, and Hubert Williams. "Police Accountability and Community Policing," U.S. Department of Justice, National Institute of Justice, November 1988.
Lyford, George J. "Boat Theft, A High-Profit/Low Risk Business," FBI Law Enforcement Bulletin, May 1982.
———. "Heavy Equipment Theft," FBI Law Enforcement Bulletin, March 1981.
Meyer, Carl H. and Stephen M. Matyas. *Cryptography: A New Dimension in Computer Data Security*, John Wiley & Sons, 1982.
Moore, Mark H. and Robert C. Trojanowicz. "Policing and the Fear of Crime," U.S. Department of Justice, National Institute of Justice, June 1988.
"National Crime Information Center (NCIC)," U.S. Department of Justice, Federal Bureau of Investigation, March 1989.
Peterson, Joseph L. "Use of Forensic Evidence by the Police and Courts," U.S. Department of Justice, National Institute of Justice, October 1987.
Rand, Michael. "Violent Crime Trends," U.S. Department of Justice, National Institute of Justice, November 1987.
"Report on the Wanted Person File Survey, April 1984," U.S. Department of Justice, FBI, NCIC, October 1984.
"Strategies for Improving Data Quality," U.S. Department of Justice, FBI, National Criminal Justice Information Policy, NCJ-111458, April 1989.

Bibliography

"Tracking Offenders, 1984." U.S. Department of Justice, National Institute of Justice, January 1988.

"The Federal Civil Justice System," U.S. Department of Justice, National Institute of Justice, Bureau of Justice Statistics Bulletin, July 1987.

Van Duyn, J. "The Human Factor in Computer Crime." Princeton, NJ: Petrocelli Books, 1985.

Wood, Udy C. "Aircraft Theft," The FBI Law Enforcement Bulletin, October 1982.

Index

A

access control, physical security, 90-96
accessed information, laws governing, 71
Adult Criminal Justice Statistical System (ACJSS), 55
applicant records, 37
applications controls, software security, 115
Area Location of Hazardous Atmospheres (ALOHA), 68
arrest, 74
art (*see* articles, identifiable)
articles, identifiable
  CJIS database, 54
  stolen/recovered, NCIC database, 15
artificial intelligence, 61-63
Automated Criminal History System (ACHS), xii, 26, 39, 55-57
Automated Criminal Intelligence Index (ACII), 58
Automated Fingerprint Identification System (AFIS), xii, 29-47, 123-125
  CAL-ID, 34-47
  latent prints, 33
  scanned images, 31-33
Automated Identification System (AIS), xi, 21-24, 27, 28
automated fingerprint reader system, 24
automated image retrieval system, 24
automated latent system model (ALSM), 23, 34
history of, 22
structure and function of, 22
automated image retrieval system (AIRS), 24
Automated Latent Print System (ALPS), 39, 40
automated latent system model (ALSM), 23-24, 34
automated teller machines, 81-82, 89
Automatic Locating Vehicle System (ALVS), 68
autos (*see* stolen/felony vehicles; recovered vehicles)

B

background investigations, personnel security, 117-118
bikes, stolen, CJIS database, 54
biometric ID system, hardware security, 103
Blair, Janet, 82-83
boats (*see* marine equipment)
Box, Judith Danelle, 102
bright line rules, 75
buildings, physical security, 89
Bundeskriminalamt (BKA), 43
Bureau of Criminal Identification (BCID), 38
Bureau of Organized Crime and Criminal Intelligence, 54

C

California Automated Identification System (CAL-ID), xii, 56, 59
Automated Latent Print System, 39
configuration of, 37
databases of, 38
digital image retrieval subs, 42
European counterpart, 43
fingerprint input, 42
fingerprint matching, 42
full use access agency (FUAA), 41
function of, 36
hardware for, 38
local input terminal (LIT), 41
process of, 35, 36
remote access network (RAN), 39
retainability of records, 37
verification only terminal (VOT), 40
Western Identification Network, 44
California Law Enforcement Telecommunications System (CLETS), xii, 4, 26, 49, 57, 59
Canadian warrants, NCIC database, 15
checks, UCAN scanning, 64
CITYPOOL, 68-69
cognitive style positioning, personnel security, 118-120
cold searches, fingerprinting, 39
cold sites, disaster recovery, 98-99
Commandants Instruction No. 1620.3, marine equipment, 12-14
common law, 75
Computer Assisted Terminal Criminal Hunt (CATCH), 69
computer crime, xiii, 79
computers (*see also* hardware security; software security)
  xii-xiv, 1, 15
  California Penal Code 499c, 72
  California Penal Code 502, 73
  Computer Security Act, 71-72
  data manipulation, 82-83
  Federal Computer Fraud and Abuse Act, 71, 72
  fraud and embezzlement, 80-82
  hardware security for, 102
  salami technique, 83

Index

computers (con't)
  scavenging, 83-84
  software piracy, 79-80
  time (logic) bomb/trap door, 85
  Trojan horse, 84
  virus or worms, 85-86
Computer Fraud and Abuse Act, 86
Computer Security Act, 71, 72
Computer-Aided Dispatching (CAD), 65-66
Computer-Aided Management of Emergency OP (CAMEO), 68
Computerized Criminal History (CCH) database, 4-5
consent, 75
construction equipment (see equipment)
contingency plans, 97-99
core, fingerprinting, 29
credit cards
  Fair Credit Reporting Act of 1975, 78
  UCAN scanning, 64
criminal history database, NCIC, 8
Criminal Identification and Information (CII) numbers, 25, 27
criminal intelligence index, 54
Criminal Justice Information Systems (CJIS), xii, 26, 39, 49-59, 114
  ACHS subsystem, 55-57, 55
  ACJSS database, 55
  automated firearms, 52
  boat/marine equipment, 53
  configuration of, 50
  databases of, 50
  organized crime database, 54, 57
  overview of, California, 50
  property/stolen bikes, 54
  stolen vehicles, 51
  wanted persons, 50
  WSIN, 57
criminal records, 37
cryptographic algorithms, 16

D

data encryption standard (DES), xiii, 105-107
data manipulation, computer crime, 82-83
decryption, 105
delta, fingerprinting, 29
detention, 74
Diffie, Whitfield, 107
digital image retrieval subsystem (DIRS), CAL-ID, 42
dignity, laws governing personal, 73
Direct Electronic Fingerprinting (DEF), 125-128
disaster recovery plans, 97-99
dispatching, Computer-aided, (CAD), 65-66

DNA matching, WIN database, 45-47
dumb terminals, 64
duplicated efforts, 2

E

electronics (see articles, identifiable)
embezzlement, computer crime, 80-82
encryption systems, xiii, 105-109
equipment (see also articles, identifiable), 15
  stolen/recovered, NCIC database, 11
exclusionary rule, 75-77
expert systems, 23, 61-63

F

Fair Credit Reporting Act of 1975, 78
farm equipment (see equipment)
FBI, National Crime Information Center (NCIC) and, 3
Federal Computer Fraud and Abuse Act, 71, 72
Fields, Ross Eugene, 81
Fifth Amendment, 76
file management
  POLICE-TRAK, 66
  Records Management and Crime Analysis System, 67
fingerprinting
  AFIS, 29-47
  classification, NCIC, 8-9
  core, 29
  delta, 29
  inkless, 41
  input, CAL-ID, 42
  latent prints, 33
  latent-cognizant techniques, 39
  matching, 30
  matching, CAL-ID, 42
  nonbookable offenses, 37
  pattern recognition techniques, 39
  recurring ridge, 29
  retainability of records and, 37
  scanned fingerprints with id system, 31-33
fire security/protection, 96-97
firearms
  automatic, CJIS database, 52
  stolen/recovered, NCIC database, 11
Fleet Management System (WHEELS), 67
Fourteenth Amendment, 76
Fourth Amendment, 73-77
fraud, computer crime, 80-82
Freedom of Information Act, 78
full use access agency (FUAA), 41

G

good faith exception, warrants, 77

H

hand print ID, hardware security, 104
hardware security, xiii, 101-109
  backup generators for electricity, 102
  biometric ID system for, 103
  encryption systems, 105-109
  finger or hand print ID, 104, 106
  magnetic-strip ID card, 103
  message authentification code (MAC), 109
  retinal pattern ID, 104
  separation of staff duties, 121
  signature analysis, 104
  terminal lock and key for, 103
  terminals and personal computers, 102
  touch pattern id, 104
  transmission security, 105
  uninterruptible power supply (UPS), 101
  voice verification systems, 104, 109
hazardous materials handling, 68
Hellman, Martin E., 107
Henry System, fingerprinting, 29, 30
Henry, Edward Richard, fingerprinting, 29
heuristics, 62
hot sites, disaster recovery, 98-99

I

image transmission devices (ITD), 41
inference, 62
inkless computer crime, 41
Intellect Investigations System, xii, 61-63
International Association of Chiefs of Police (IACP), 3
International Law Enforcement Telecommunications System (INLETS), xii, 4, 26, 49, 58
Interstate Identification Index (Triple I), xi, 21, 24-28
  privacy and security issues, 28
  structure and function, 26
  users and use of, 27-28

J

jewelry (see articles, identifiable)

L

LandTrak, 65
latent prints, 33
latent-cognizant techniques, fingerprinting, 39
Law Enformcement Telecommunications Systems (LETS), xii, 58-59

140

Index

Lewis, Lloyd Benjamin, 81
license plates, stolen, NCIC database, 14
Lifescan, xiv
local automated Fingerprint Identification System (LAFIS), 41
local input terminal (LIT), CAL-ID, 41
logic bomb, computer crime, 85

M

magnetic-strip id card, hardware security, 103
mapping, LandTrak, 65
marine equipment
 CJIS database, 53
 stolen/recovered, NCIC database, 12-14
Marshall, Sammy, 81
Master Name Index (MNI), xii, 39, 55-57
Message Authentication Code (MAC), xiii, 109
Missing Childrens Act of 1982, 6
missing/unidentified persons
 disabled persons, 7
 endangered, 7
 involuntary, 8
 juveniles, 8
 NCIC database, 6-8
Morris, Robert Jr., 86
MOTION network, New Orleans traffic control, 69

N

National Bureau of Standards (NBS), 106
National Crime Information Center (NCIC), xi, 3-19, 25, 26, 27, 28, 49, 59, 114
 AIS subsystem, 21-24
 Canadian warrants, 15
 CCH database, 4-5
 criminal history database, 8
 databases of, 5-16
 fingerprint classification, 8-9
 history of, 4-5
 information storage/dissemination, 4
 long-range goals of, 18-19
 missing/unidentified persons, 6-8
 mode of operation, 16-17
 on-line status of, 4
 originating agency id file, 16
 probable cause and, 10
 quality control steps, 17
 recoverd vehicles, 10
 security and privacy issues, 18
 stolen license plates, 14
 stolen/felony vehicles, 9-10
 stolen/recovered articles, 15
 stolen/recovered firearms, 11
 stolen/recovered heavy equipment, 11
 stolen/recovered marine, 12-14
 stolen/recovered securities, 14
 Triple I subsystem, 24-28
 US Secret Service protective file, 16
 wanted persons, 5-6
NLETS, 4, 25, 26, 49, 58
nonbookable offenses, 37

O

optical character readers (OCR), 24
organized crime databases, xii, 54, 57
originating agency ID file, NCIC database, 16
overlapping responsibilities, 2

P

parking lots, physical security, 89
passwords, software security, 114
pattern recognition techniques, computer crime, 39
personnel security, xiv, 117-122
 background investigations, 117-118
 discontented employees, signs of, 120-121
 enforcing policies for, 122
 orientation for new officers, 121
 personnel follow-up, 118-120
 separation of duties, computer staff, 121
physical security, xiii, 87-99
 access control, 90-96
 building and parking lots, 89
 contingency plans for, 97-99
 disaster recovery plans, 97-99
 fire security/protection, 96-97
 hot vs. cold sites, 98-99
 risk analysis, 87-92
piracy, software, 79-80
plain text, 105
POLICE-TRAK, 66
Privacy Act of 1974, 77
privacy laws, 73
private key approach, data encryption, 106
probable cause, 10, 73, 74
protected witnesses, NCIC database for, 16
public key encryption (PKE), xiii, 105, 107-109
Public Record Act, 73

R

rap sheet, 22
records (see file management)
Records Management and Crime Analysis System, 67
recovered vehicles, NCIC database, 10-11
recurving ridge, fingerprinting, 29
redundant process, 2
remote access network (RAN), CAL-ID, 39
Resource Access Control Facility (RACF), xiii, 112-114
retainability of records, 37
retinal patterns, hardware security, 104
Rifkin, Stanley Mark, 92-95
risk analysis, physical security, 87-92

S

salami technique, computer crime, 83
scavenging, computer crime, 83-84
search and seizure, 74
Secret Service protective file, NCIC database, 16
securities (see stocks and bonds)
security, 73
signature analysis, hardware security, 104
smart terminals, 64
software piracy, 79-80
software security (see also computer crime), xiii, 111-115
 agency security policy and control procedures, 111-112
 applications controls, 115
 passwords, 114
 protection levels of, 111
 Resource Access Control Facility (RACF), 112-114
 separation of staff duties, 121
 systems and programming standards, 114
State Identification (SID) numbers, 25, 27
Station for Atmospheric Monitoring (SAM), 68
stocks and bonds,
 stolen/recovered, NCIC database, 14
stolen/felony vehicles
 CJIS database, 51
 NCIC database, 9-10

T

ten-print cards, fingerprinting, 29
terminal lock and key, hardware security, 103
time bomb, computer crime, 85
touch pattern id, hardware security, 104
transmission security, hardware security, 105
trap door, computer crime, 85
Trojan horse, computer crime, 84

U

uninterruptible power supply (UPS), xiii, 101

Index

United Crime Alert Network (UCAN), xii, 64
United Crime Reports (UCR), 68

V

vehicles
  automatic locating system (ALVS), 68
  fleet management (WHEELS), 67
  verification only terminal (VOT),

CAL-ID, 40
virus, computer crime, 85-86
voice print, hardware security, 104
voice verification systems, hardware security, 109

W

wanted persons
  CJIS database, 50-51
  NCIC database, 5-6
Western Identification Network

(WIN), xii, xiv, 44-47, 123-124
  DNA database for, 45-47
Western States Information Network (WSIN), xii, 54, 57-58
WHEELS fleet management system, 67
Wire Fraud Statue, 71-72
Wyche, Barry, 84

Z

Zinn, H.D., 86